MARK BUCHANAN

God Walk

MOVING AT THE SPEED OF YOUR SOUL

ZONDERVAN
BOOKS

ZONDERVAN BOOKS

God Walk
Copyright © 2020 by Mark Buchanan

Requests for information should be addressed to:
Zondervan, 3900 Sparks Dr. SE, Grand Rapids, Michigan 49546

Zondervan titles may be purchased in bulk for educational, business, fundraising, or sales promotional use. For information, please email SpecialMarkets@Zondervan.com.

ISBN 978-0-310-29366-8 (hardcover)
ISBN 978-0-310-35584-7 (audio)
ISBN 978-0-310-41331-8 (ebook)
ISBN 978-0-310-36089-6 (international trade paper edition)

Published in association with the literary agency of Ann Spangler and Company, 1420 Pontiac Road SE, Grand Rapids, MI 49506.

Cover design: Studio Gearbox
Cover illustration: Kevin Hill Illustration | Shutterstock
Author photo: Sarah Buchanan Photography
Interior design: Denise Froehlich

Printed in the United States of America

20 21 22 23 24 25 /LSC/ 10 9 8 7 6 5 4 3 2 1

I dedicate this book to my parents,
Bruce and Joyce Buchanan,
who taught me how to walk.

Other Books by Mark Buchanan

David: Rise (a novel)

Hidden in Plain Sight: The Secret of More

The Holy Wild: Trusting in the Character of God

The Rest of God: Restoring Your Soul by Restoring Sabbath

Spiritual Rhythm: Being with Jesus Every Season of Your Soul

Things Unseen: Living in Light of Forever

Your Church Is Too Safe: Why Following Christ Turns the World Upside-Down

Your God Is Too Safe: Rediscovering the Wonder of a God You Can't Control

God Walk

Via Dolorosa in Jerusalem, retracing a few miles from *The Pilgrim's Progress*, or walking in the footsteps of Abraham, Jesus' disciples, and the lame man. Here is a chance to look at our walk with God as pedestrians rather than motorists.

—LEE ECLOV, pastor; author, *Feels Like Home: How Rediscovering the Church as Family Changes Everything*

With his trademark lilt and languorous style, Mark Buchanan saunters, but never rambles, down an ancient track nearly lost to the Christian tradition. His is an invitation not to get in more steps but to slowly walk with God himself. This book is a good gift to the global church.

—JARED BROCK, author, *A Year of Living Prayerfully*

When you go for a walk in the wilderness, it really helps to have a guide who has walked the way before. For almost twenty years, Mark's words have served as a trusted guide helping me avoid pits and cul-de-sacs, and have encouraged me to keep on when I've become disheartened. That this book is literally and metaphorically about walking makes it all the more helpful and appropriate for today. To quote Mark (who is quoting Tolkien's Samwise), "I will go with you" is the most helpful, comforting sentence one could ever hear, especially when the speaker follows through and does just that. All Mark's books have been like that for me; his wisdom and shepherd's heart have often been my traveling companions. Thank you, Mark, for going with us wherever our feet fall and helping us remember that we are not alone.

—BRIAN DOERKSEN, songwriter; recording artist

In this beautiful, inspiring book, Mark shows us how the simple rhythm of walking can take us farther on the path of wholeness, joy, and God than we imagined possible. Poetic, poignant, and immensely practical, this book will change your life . . . one step at a time.

—KEN SHIGEMATSU, pastor, Tenth Church, Vancouver;
bestselling author, *Survival Guide for the Soul*

Oh, Buchanan and his sly genius. He is at once eloquent and earthy, challenging and comforting, prophetic and funny, and totally in cahoots with the Holy Spirit. In this book, Buchanan somehow makes an assault on our hurry-sickness feel like a long, restorative walk with a really good friend.

—CAROLYN ARENDS, recording artist; author;
director of education, Renovaré

Mark Buchanan wants us to actually walk—to put one foot in front of the other, and do it often—because walking can be spiritual exercise. "Walking," he says, "is the way we keep pace with the three-mile-an-hour God. It is God speed." This book has the feel of strolling down the paths of, say, Spain's Santiago El Camino pilgrimage or the

What can I say about this book? There is so much to say! Literary masterpiece, written in prose full of energy and light. Contagiously fresh. Invitingly deep. On and on. The stuff of spiritual classics. Why are you able to write such a brilliant book, Mark? Because you actually live what you write. You walk. And walk. With God. At God speed. On the way. *Via dolorosa*, the path that leads to resurrection living. Thank you for taking me on the walk and teaching me how to walk better. I wish I lived closer to you so I could walk with you. Your book will have to do for now. And it does. Thank you.

—DARRELL JOHNSON, retired pastor and professor;
speaker; author, *The Glory of Preaching*;
mentor; grandfather; lover of long walks

Mark Buchanan has done it again—written something for one and all that is thoughtful, compelling, and practical: this is essential reading for those keen to come to a greater appreciation of the interplay between the interior life and our bodies.

—GORDON T. SMITH, president and professor
of systematic and spiritual theology, Ambrose
University; author, *The Voice of Jesus*

Walking is as natural as wind or sky or breath. However, most of us engage in walking functionally and forcefully, moving swiftly from one location to another. The garage. The basement. The office. The sea. The mountain. The sanctuary. Thankfully, Mark Buchanan arrests us in our trek and invites us to slow down and notice our strides, our hearts, our pathways, and our destinations. At God speed, we listen, we remember, we heal, and we renew. Walk with God and be transformed.

—STEPHEN A. MACCHIA, founder and president,
Leadership Transformations; director, Pierce
Center at Gordon-Conwell Theological Seminary;
author, *Becoming a Healthy Church*

Contents

MILE THREE: PRESSING ON

God walks "slowly" because he is love. If he is not love he would move much faster. Love has its speed. It is an inner speed. It is a spiritual speed. It is a different kind of speed from the technological speed to which we are accustomed. It is "slow" and yet it is lord over all the other speeds since it is the speed of love. It goes on in the depths of our life whether we notice it or not.

—KOSUKE KOYAMA, *THREE MILE AN HOUR GOD*

MILE ONE

SETTING OUT

"Leave your simple ways and you will live;
walk in the way of insight."

—PROVERBS 9:6

CHAPTER 1

Three Miles an Hour

My friend Norm can't walk.

He once could, with poise, with strength. He wasn't Buster Keaton, but he strode the earth with vigor and ease and effortless balance. But in as much time as it takes you to read this sentence, he stopped walking. Not by choice. He lost the use of both legs, and most of the use of both arms, when his horse, his trusted horse, threw him sideways and gravity pulled him earthward and he hit the ground at an angle that broke things inside him. In a blink, he went from agility to paralysis, from mobility to confinement, from standing most days to sitting all of them. One moment, his legs went wherever he told them. The next, they refused.

Norm once walked all the time but never much thought about it. He never contemplated the simple joy, the giddy freedom, the everyday magic of walking: to bound up or down a flight of stairs, to glide across a kitchen floor, to stroll a beach, to hike a trail. To move from here to there on nothing more than his own two legs, under his own locomotion. Now, Norm thinks about walking all the time. He watches others do it—*Uprights*, he calls them—bounding, gliding, strolling, hiking, and the dozens of other things most of us do with our legs with barely a thought about it. It stuns and saddens him. He would give almost anything to walk again, and if ever by some miracle of heaven or earth his capacity is restored, it's almost all he will ever do.

My friend Norm can't walk, but he thinks about it a lot.

Until recently, I was the opposite: I walked a lot but thought about it almost never.

Walking is, along with eating and sleeping, our most practiced human activity. But unlike eating and sleeping, we don't need to do it to survive. And so walking, though our most practiced human activity, is maybe our most taken-for-granted one, and sometimes our most neglected. You can, after all, go only seconds without breathing, mere days without eating. But walking—you can pass an entire lifetime and still do little of that.

Until recently, I had lost, if ever I possessed, sheer astonishment at the simple, humble miracle of carrying myself every day everywhere. These legs are more wondrous than a magic carpet, more regal than a king's palanquin. But only now have I come to see it.

THE SPEED OF OUR SOULS

Everyone who can walk walks, even the most sedentary, if only from bed to couch, from table to fridge, from desk to copier. We walk, for the most part, because we can't help it—because an escalator or elevator or car or plane or train or golf cart is unavailable. We walk up and down stairs. We walk the lengths of hallways. We walk through malls. We walk from curbsides to restaurants, from parking lots to clothing stores. "Walking," Evan Esar says, "isn't a lost art: one must, by some means, get to the garage."[1]

Most of us walk unthinkingly, without gratitude, maybe even resentfully. Our walking is accidental, incidental, inevitable, maybe grudging. It's what we do between sitting.

But not all of us. Some of us walk because it's magic and beautiful and mysterious and sometimes dangerous. We walk because we see things differently when we walk. We feel more deeply, think more clearly. We walk to figure things out. We walk to sort ourselves out. We walk to get in shape. We walk to get a sense of the scale of things—the bigness of trees, the smallness of beetles, the real distance between places. We walk because we experience land and sky and light in fresh ways—in ways, I am tempted to say, closer to reality.

We walk because three miles an hour, as the writer Rebecca Solnit says, is about the speed of thought,[2] and maybe the speed of our souls. We walk because if we go much faster for much longer, we'll start to lose ourselves: our bodies will atrophy, our thinking will jumble, our very souls will wither.

Do you not feel this?

I do.

I walk because three miles an hour seems to be the pace God keeps. It's God speed.

A PHYSICAL DISCIPLINE

The seed of this book was annoyance, or grief, or something in between. I was annoyed or grieved or whatever it is that lies between that many spiritual traditions have a corresponding physical discipline and Christianity has none. Hinduism has yoga. Taoism has tai chi. Shintoism has karate. Buddhism has kung fu. Confucianism has hapkido. Sikhism has gatka.

Christianity has nothing.

This is odd. The very core of Christian faith is incarnation— God's coming among us as one of us to walk with us. Incarnation is Christianity's flesh and blood. And every part of Christian faith seeks embodiment, a way of being lived out here, now, in person. The church has fought tenaciously against anything that contradicts this. The earliest, most noxious, and most persistent heresy of authentic Christian faith is Gnosticism. Gnosticism says the body doesn't matter—or worse, it's evil. It's a thing to be despised, maybe used, maybe indulged, but eventually discarded. It has no inherent value.

Gnosticism is incarnation's mortal enemy.

Christianity insists that the Word became flesh and dwelt among us, walked among us. And it insists that all words, all ideas, all theories, all theologies, all doctrines must become flesh and dwell among us. It calls us to walk out our faith, not just know it or speak it or argue it.

So it's odd: that a faith so insistent on these things, a faith so inescapably incarnational, never developed a matching physical discipline to help its followers yoke their faith to practice: body to mind, holiness to breath, thought to movement, the inward to the outward.

Very odd.

Except, did it? Did Christian faith have a corresponding physical discipline, then lost it?

That's what I'm going to argue here. And I'm going to argue that this discipline is the oldest and simplest practice around.

It's walking.

It started very early with a God in the habit of walking in the garden in the cool of the day. Likely, he invited our first parents to join him, until that terrible day they ran away and hid instead. (See Gen. 3:8.) Even after that, holiness and walking with God were the same thing. "Enoch walked with God . . . Noah . . . walked with God" (Gen. 5:22; 6:9).

Later, the prophet Micah asks, What does God require of you? He considers a list of religious options: extravagant worship, costly sacrifice. But no. It's simple and personal: God wants us to love mercy and to do justly. And then Micah throws in a third thing, or maybe it's the one thing needed, the single activity that makes the other two possible: "to walk humbly with your God" (Mic. 6:6–8).

Later still, the peripatetic apostle Paul picks up the theme. "Follow God's example, therefore, as dearly loved children," he exhorts the Ephesians. "Walk in the way of love, just as Christ loved us and gave himself up for us as a fragrant offering and sacrifice to God" (Eph. 5:1–2).

Walking is a primary way of knowing God.

GOD SPEED

This is a book about walking. Particularly, it's a book about walking as spiritual formation and spiritual discipline. In its pages, I explore many things—walking as healing, walking as exercise, walking as exorcism, walking as prayer, walking as remembering, walking as pilgrimage, walking as suffering and friendship and attentiveness. I am interested not so much in heroic or historic walking—pilgrimages, great marches, huge feats of endurance

through parched wastelands or dense forests or precarious mountain passes—as in the ordinary, unsung walking most of us do
every day. I'm interested in the simple, humble miracle of carrying ourselves around. I'm interested in the spirituality of walking,
in the deep-down good it does us even when we're not trying to
derive any benefit from it.

Each chapter has a companion, a brief reflection on some
theme emerging from the chapter, and ending, explicitly or
implicitly, with a call to action (or inaction). I am calling these
companion pieces "God Speed." Because always, I circle back
to one grand theme: walking is the way we keep pace with the
three-mile-an-hour God. It is God speed. We walk with a God
who seems in no particular hurry and who, it seems, enjoys the
going there as much as the getting there. A God who is slow.
This is a book about being alongside the God who, incarnate in
Jesus, turns to us as he passes by—on foot, always on foot—and
says, simply and subversively, "Come, follow me."

Come, walk with me.

This book is about hearing this invitation as more than a
metaphor. It is about working out on the ground, on the way,
our friendship with God, and with ourselves and with others
and with the good and fragile earth that holds us up and marks
our steps.

SEVEN MILES WITH A STRANGER

Luke tells a story near the end of his gospel about two people
walking and talking, trying to work out what's happened to
them. One's named Cleopas, the other we don't know. They
are traveling from Jerusalem to "a village called Emmaus, about

seven miles [away]." At three miles an hour, that's more than a two-hour walk.

A long time to talk.

A long time to think.

Enough time to change your mind.

Enough time to have your world turned upside down.

Cleopas and his companion—some think it was his wife or one of his children—are disciples of Jesus. Or had been. They are crushed by disappointment: Jesus is dead. Killed. Crucified. Before their very eyes. Unmistakable. Undeniable. Irreversible. Everything they had believed about Jesus has been proven false. Their words tell the story: "We had hoped that he was the one who was going to redeem Israel" (Luke 24:21).

We *had hoped*. That he *was*.

Past tense. The swan song of the defeated, the coda of the brokenhearted.

As they walk, a man joins them. He walks with them. He is an unusual traveler. A bit odd, maybe a tad thick: he seems clueless about the events that have shattered these two people's world and have gripped and rocked an entire nation. This traveler doesn't seem to know a thing about Jesus—his life, his words, his works. His brutal messy death. Or anything about a strange rumor going around—angels, an empty tomb, the dead raised.

Then the stranger starts to talk.

It turns out, even if he doesn't seem to be up on recent news, he does know a lot of Scripture. And he knows a lot about the great hope of the Scriptures, the promised Messiah. As they walk, he talks. He teaches Cleopas and his companion about how all roads, all Scripture, lead to the same place: the Messiah will suffer before he enters his glory.

At last, they reach Emmaus. The traveler tries to take his leave. He seems to have farther to go. But Cleopas and the other disciple are having none of it: "They urged him strongly, 'Stay with us, for it is nearly evening; the day is almost over'" (Luke 24:29).

So the stranger relents, enters their home. They serve him a meal. Then he does something very odd for a guest in someone else's home: he takes charge. "When he was at the table with them, he took bread, gave thanks, broke it and began to give it to them" (v. 30).

And that's when it happens—"their eyes were opened and they recognized him" (v. 31). He inexplicably vanishes at that very moment. But it's okay. It's enough. They know who he is. They've seen this very thing before—taking bread, giving thanks, breaking bread, giving bread.

This is the signature—even more than his Bible teaching—of the very Jesus they thought was dead: taking, thanking, breaking, giving. It's Jesus.

All this happens at the table. But the long walk isn't beside the point. It isn't wasted breath.

It is preparation.

"Were not our hearts burning within us," they ask each other, "while he talked with us on the road and opened the Scriptures to us?" (v. 32).

This—like so many stories in Scripture—is both about other people and about us. It is about these two people, one named Cleopas, who lived long ago, far away. It's about their discovering Jesus present with them even as they lament his absence.

But it's also about us. It's our story. Jesus keeps doing this, becoming present with us even as we lament his absence. He keeps showing up, showing us things, walking beside us, making our hearts burn within us. We might not recognize him at the time. That often comes later.

And it usually takes some walking to get there.

I started this book in a place I often visit, usually to write. It's called Fireweed: a private retreat house on twenty-six secluded acres. It is ringed with deep coastal woods, and on its eastern side lie sloping fields of tall wild grasses. In the middle of the property is a marshy lake plied by three families of beavers, who come out at dawn and dusk and swim in leisurely circles or zigzags, and slap their tails hard and loud on the glassy water, to spook the fish, I guess. Or maybe to entertain me, which is a theory I'm quite attached to. In the spring and summer and fall—I write this in the early days of winter, nudging right up against Christmas—the lake's edge is laced with lily pads, preternaturally green, many of them supporting the weight of a frog camouflaged to match its habitat. Each frog sits in perfect stillness, sometimes for hours, waiting for a winged whirring buzzing thing to fly within reach of its blindingly quick and sticky tongue. The reeds circling the lake are haloed with dragon and damsel flies, and all manner of birds flit or perch or wade round about.

It is a small and perfect paradise.

Each day I'm here, I walk the land. A trail encircles most of the property's edges (the marsh at the western edge is impassable), and many other trails crisscross through its forests and fields. I walk most of these trails most days. It maybe takes an hour, more or less, depending on my mood, the weather, how sodden the low places are, what catches my eye. I must have walked this land, some length and breadth of it, in some order, fifty times. Every time, it becomes a little more familiar, a muscle memory, a room in my heart. And yet every time it holds fresh discoveries, like a place I have never been before and couldn't have imagined. Walking deepens the familiar and yet keeps revealing the new.

ATTENTIVE TO NUDGES

The seed of this book, I already said, was annoyance. But the catalyst for it was something else: the suspicion that when the Bible talks about walking in the Spirit or walking in the light or walking in truth and so on, it means this in more than a figurative way. My suspicion was that Paul and John, and others, meant it equally in a literal way. After all, these were people who walked. Paul especially. He covered a lot of ground on foot. Someone has calculated that his missionary travels alone covered ten thousand miles. So when he exhorts, say, the church in Galatia to keep in step with the Spirit, it's likely that his exhortation is rooted in his actual experience. "As you walk," he is saying, "from your house to your neighbor's house, or from this town to that town, do as I do: be attentive to the nudges and whispers of God's Spirit. Be listening and speaking to the one who walks with you. Follow his lead."

When Paul visited Athens, he "walked around and looked carefully at [their] objects of worship" (Acts 17:23). He was attentive to the spiritual condition of people in that city, to this man's beliefs, that woman's practices. Especially, he was attentive to the way each man's and each woman's spirituality congealed into a zeitgeist, a spirit of the age, an overall mood. If one person believes something deeply, it hardly registers. But if a million people believe it, it takes on a shape, a weight, a force. Paul felt in Athens the weight of what the people there believed. It bothered him what he saw, what he felt. Actually, earlier, he kind of pitched a fit over it: "While Paul was waiting for them in Athens, he was greatly distressed to see that the city was full of idols" (Acts 17:16). Greatly distressed: in the Greek, it means he could hardly breathe.

But he kept walking, walking around, looking at everything. Thinking, praying. Maybe, in his walking around, he remembered what his fellow apostle once said, "how God anointed Jesus of Nazareth with the Holy Spirit and power, and how he *went around doing good* and healing all who were under the power of the devil, because God was with him" (Acts 10:38, emphasis mine). Jesus never pitched a fit over people's spiritual condition. Rather, he loaded up with divine power and set out with healing in his wings. Jesus went on a mission of restoration and liberation. Was Paul remembering that? Is that what helped him recover from his own little pharisaical hangover? At any rate, by the time Paul gets up to talk to the Athenian elite down at the Philosophers' Club, he's in a much better mood. He sees that, underneath the Athenians' distressing idolatry, is a deep longing, a holy hunger, a searching for the God who is as close as breath and ready, at the slightest prompting, to turn to each and all with healing in his wings.

All's to say, I am pretty sure walking is how Paul largely worked out his faith. He kept God speed. In this, he would have simply been following a habit so ingrained it was second nature.

Indeed, the earliest name for Christianity was the Way, suggesting that it was not a set of doctrines to master but a path to travel. Suggesting that each step was a deepening of the familiar and a discovery of the new.

I picture Paul, say, after he saw the vision of a man from Macedonia, making his way up the coast from Troas to Philippi, sometimes traveling by boat, but otherwise on foot, hobbling and lurching on those bandy legs he was rumored to have. Luke is with him, and Silas. A few others. Sometimes, especially when rain falls hard and slanting, they walk in brooding silence, their faces deep in the tunnels of their hoods, each dreaming of warmth and food. But then one of them says, "The farmers need this rain. It is God's grace." And then they all remember all the ways God's grace is being poured out.

But it doesn't rain much in those parts, so usually they walk on the shady side of the road and talk of everything—people they know, hopes they cherish, places they've been, things they've seen. Likely they talk about things they've read or heard read aloud. But always their talk circles back to this one thing: Christ, his life and death and resurrection and priestly ministry, and all the ways he's changed everything. This is never far from their thoughts or lips or hearts.

Each step is a deepening of the familiar and a discovery of the new.

All of it at roughly three miles an hour. God speed.

God Speed

WALKING FAITHFULLY

In the beginning, we walked.

In the cool of the day. In the shade of the garden. With slow animals and fast ones, cheetahs and tortoises; with docile beasts and wild ones, cows and wolves; with creatures that bounded and others that lumbered, with ones that scuttled and others that waddled. The tiger could rend and devour us, except it didn't, except it pressed its huge head against our hip and stretched its neck out for us to scratch and made a sound of deep contentment in its throat. The chicken eventually bored us—we found it too dull, too pedestrian, too unexotic, to stir our wonder—but that first time we set eyes on it and had to think up its name, we nearly fell over from shock.

And we walked with each other. Hand in hand, I'm pretty sure. Whispering, though no one was eavesdropping. Or so we thought.

And we walked with God.

We walked with God. Talking with him as though he were one of us, one with us, God among us: a brother, a friend, a confidant. A fellow pedestrian.

It was all good, so very good. There was night, and there was day. And each new morning, we rose and walked again.

And then it all went tragically awry.

Here, I think, is the saddest line ever written: "Then the man and his wife heard the sound of the LORD God as he was walking in the garden in the cool of the day, and they hid from the LORD God" (Gen. 3:8).

And they hid.

We've been hiding ever since, wary, skittish, hugging the shadows. Wearing disguises. Watching the exits. We have all become like Cain, restless wanderers (Gen. 4:12), though many of us are sedentary versions of this, restless and listless both. But we're never quite at home.

The story doesn't end there, though. It hardly begins there: before the story is barely underway, we come upon one of the most hopeful lines ever written: "When Enoch had lived sixty-five years, he became the father of Methuselah. After he became the father of Methuselah, Enoch walked faithfully with God three hundred years and had other sons and daughters. Altogether, Enoch lived a total of 365 years. Enoch walked faithfully with God; then he was no more, because God took him away" (Gen. 5:21–24).

Walking with God, walking faithfully with God, returns. Soon after stumbling, we hit our stride again.

Well, I suppose if at sixty-five I got the news I was about to become a father, I might start walking with God too. People then, of course, enjoyed (or endured) extraordinary longevity, and sixty-five was no more than early adolescence. But the news that he was about to become a father at age sixty-five must have hit Enoch in much the same way the news that I was about to become a father hit me at age thirty: *Oh my God!*

For Enoch, for me, that exclamation was literal and visceral. A child is coming, and I'm not ready. Not equal to the

task. This is bigger than me. My soul is too shallow, my stock-
pile of wisdom too scant, my ego too fragile, my resources too
meager.

O my God!

And so I did the same thing Enoch does. It's the same
thing many of us do, however haltingly, however awkwardly,
when we learn we're in the thick of matters too large for us: we
walk with God. We need more than ourselves for these things.
Some tasks are too daunting, too vital, too big, too messy for
our own strength or wisdom to handle.

And just so, walking with God returns soon after it goes
missing. But now a new thing comes into play: faithfulness.
Now we must want it, choose it, seek it. Now we must outwit
our reluctance or inertia. Now walking with God becomes a
discipline, something good but hard. We are invited to say yes
to it daily, hourly even. Now we must show up to walk with
God like all the world depends on it.

Which, in a way, it does.

And just so, the language of walking—walking with God,
walking in the light, walking in truth, walking in holiness,
keeping in step with the Holy Spirit, and suchlike—laces like
footprints all through the Bible, start to finish. It is, as I say
in the first chapter, the one physical discipline that the Bible
consistently associates with a life of faith. It's so common it's
almost pedestrian.

For your first God Speed, why not reclaim what you
might have lost or forgotten or maybe never knew: make
walking with God the center of your life. Why not choose

deep companionship with the three-mile-an-hour God? Bring everything to him, every last little thing, like a child brings her art from school to show her parents. Especially, bring yourself to God, every last little bit of yourself, no matter how strong the impulse to hide.

I recommend, for your first walk, that you go slow. Take a long time, even if you go only a short distance.

Here he comes, walking toward you in the cool—or heat—of the day.

Do you hear that? He's calling you.

Go. Go.

CHAPTER 2

How I Learned to Walk

I was up on my feet early, at ten months. A kinetic wonder-boy, me, always on the move. Wanderlust claimed me early and sent me forth. I remember some of my early childhood. I remember, for instance, at eighteen months cutting myself badly crawling out of my crib. Before I turned four, I set off on several self-appointed adventures. I crossed, without supervision, and more than once, the busy road in front of our house, just to gaze on the swift blue-green river that flowed below the cutbanks. I hunted down, while my father watched sports on TV, my ever-vanishing mother. It took me all the way to the neighborhood grocery store many blocks away. After a bath, I routinely leaped up from the water and, before my mother could capture my dripping slippery body, bolted outside in all my glorious nakedness and ran laps around the yard.

And so on.

We moved when I was five, and it was then my older brother and I began walking in wilderness. Our wilderness was only a canyon with a creek a few hundred yards from our house. But at that age, it may as well have been a cracked dry lakebed in the Navajo desert or a vast tract of arboreal forest in the mountains of Russia or a tangled pathless swath of jungle in the Amazon. It was populated with coyotes, cougars, rattlesnakes, and suchlike, not to mention bloodsucking ticks, so things could have gone terribly wrong. But most weekends, there we were, my brother and I, just the two of us or maybe we brought a friend, exploring that canyon's twists and turns and, near its end where a rock wall ran straight up, venturing into a low-ceilinged cave that had a sharp bend twenty feet down, though we never got up enough courage to go past that bend.

When I was seven, we moved again, far north, to a place where winter came early and stayed late. The town gave way at its border to real wilderness. My brother and I walked into that wilderness many Saturdays, from early spring to late fall. We had our father drop us off at the edge of the forest, and off we'd go, like two innocents in a German folktale, with neither map nor compass and with just enough food and water to get us through the day. Sometimes we had to wade through snow past our waists. Once we found an abandoned mill and, beside its rusting saws and motors, a mound of sawdust thirty feet high. We climbed and rolled down it, over and over, and then spent a night in an anguish of burning itches, like being devoured by fire ants. A few times we got plenty lost and openly worried that we wouldn't make it back by nightfall, or at all.

I've been on my feet a long time.

But only now, as I confessed in the opening chapter, have I started to really think about walking, the gift of it, the miracle of it, the beauty of it. I have gone places on just these two legs and these two feet, with their intricacy of small bones, that almost defies reason: far and near, up and down, back and forth, here and there. I carried myself the whole way.

Even when I drive my car or ride my motorcycle or pedal my bike, at some moment in every journey, even if just to the mailbox or corner store, I reach the point past which no manmade thing can carry me an inch farther. Then my own body must take over. Then I must carry myself.

It's a miracle.

Maybe the closest we ever get to spontaneously recognizing this miracle, with the awe and joy equal to the thing, is when a child—especially *our* child—takes her first step: this little one who until now we carried in our arms is suddenly carrying herself. At first she trembles above the floor as though hovering over an abyss. She wavers between fear and anticipation, feeling the treachery of gravity, the dizzying power of great heights, but also the thrill of freedom.

Just give her a few days, she'll be blazing about the place, as pleased with herself as anyone ever felt winning or conquering, and maybe a bit more.

She's learned to walk.

BASIC INSTINCT

But does anyone actually ever *learn* to walk?

Isn't walking something we can't help? A basic instinct, potent and ancient, takes over. We can't resist it. It's a wild thing in us, irresistible. Our genetic coding—and, I think, the fact that we are made in the image of the God who once walked with us in the cool of the day and who came to earth to walk with us again—lays hold of us, and we're up and at it. Parents, older siblings, aunts, uncles, neighbors even: all coax our walking, cheer and clap at the first signs of it. Soon after, our parents brood over our every step lest we fall headlong down the stairs or crack our heads open on the corner of the glass table. Later still, they worry about the paths we walk.

But it's not as if anyone *teaches* us to walk. That's in our seed. It emerges naturally, as noses lump out on our faces, as teeth blade out from our gums, as hair sprouts from our scalps (and then, alas for some of us, molts forever).

We can't help but walk.

Maybe that's why, after our families' initial enthusiasm over our first steps, few of us think much about it. We seldom ponder—philosophically, theologically, existentially—the fact of walking any more than we ponder the fact that we have noses or teeth or hair. We usually ponder the fact of walking (or the fact that we have a nose or teeth or hair) only when it goes missing, stops working. We ponder these things in their absence or diminishment, but not in their flourishing.

A twelve-year-old boy who runs like a gazelle might delight in his legs' and body's prowess, but he rarely reflects on these things. Only when he breaks his leg and must hobble around the house all summer on crutches and watch his friends do things now forbidden him does he turn his full attention to the miracle of what he's lost.

WHICH WAY?

We don't learn to walk. We just do it and don't give it much mind until something forces us to stop.

But we do learn which *way* to walk. We learn which roads

to travel. That takes some instruction and no little amount of pondering. Few of us inherit a good sense of which way to go. We don't come by direction naturally, at least not in the same way we come by our eye color or skin tone or the texture of our voices. We don't grow, as a matter of course, into any sure, clear knowing of which paths to take, which ones to avoid. For that, we need instruction. And we need no little amount of pondering.

Recently I traveled to Europe with two friends, Kevin and Craig. Both were fine company. Craig especially was a fun and enthusiastic travel companion—curious, easily delighted, chatty, insightful. He was in an almost constant state of childlike astonishment at every last little thing: not just the Eiffel Tower or Big Ben or the Louvre or Edinburgh Castle but cobblestone streets and Tudor houses and old ruins and cows grazing. He helped me recover a sense of wonder and thankfulness and to shed several layers of cynicism.

But Craig had little sense—actually, none at all—of direction. He got lost just going around the block. He was nearly always bewildered about where we were. "Is it that way?" he'd ask. It never was. "No," Kevin or I would answer, "it's that way," and point in the opposite direction.

I should mention for the sake of kindness and fairness that I had three clear advantages. One, I obsess over which way we're going, a trait that comes from being lost too many times. Two, I had downloaded a map into my phone and, when confused, pulled it up to get my bearings. And three, I had several times before been in most of the towns and cities we visited, and I had walked them all. Indeed, the first time I'd been in each place, I was pretty much as turned-around and bewildered as Craig.

But the whole experience made me realize afresh that knowing which way to go is not instinctual. We're taught it. We're tutored in it. We seek maps and guides for it. We ponder it.

Walk this way. That's a biblical refrain. It implies that there are many ways to walk, some that may not turn out well. Some trails on the landscape lead to good places, some not. It's also true of life. *Walk this way* is an invitation to travel on a path that leads to a good place.

THE WAY

I had to learn to walk in this sense. For my first twenty years, I walked in a way that seemed good to me. But increasingly, I felt lost. I was lost. I was going nowhere, and fast. When I was twenty-one, I began to follow Christ. I still didn't know where I was going. Still don't. But I had a guide who kept saying, *Come, follow me. Walk this way.* When I'd ask him, *Where, exactly?* he'd only smile, enigmatically, and keep walking. Slowly, slowly, I learned to trust him. He seemed to have a good sense of direction.

The early church got this. They referred to the faith, and maybe to Christ himself, as the Way. Christians were followers of the Way (Acts 9:2; 19:23; 24:14, 22). In John's gospel, Jesus tells his disciples that he is the way, the truth, and the life (John 14:6). John wasn't written until nearly the end of the first century, but the church was using this language before that, probably during the ministry of Jesus. The first Christians, after all, heard Jesus say "I am the way" long before John wrote down those words.

The Way. Not the Idea. Not the Ideal. Not the Doctrine. Not the Philosophy. Not the Moral Teaching. Not the Institution.

The Way.

Author and business guru Peter Senge once spoke to a gathering of pastors, not his normal audience. Early in the day, he went to a bookstore and checked out the Christian spirituality section, not his normal reading. He noticed that books on Buddhism—Senge practices Zen Buddhism—outnumbered books on Christianity five to one. That evening, when he got up to speak to the pastors, he mentioned this and asked if any of them wondered why this was so. He gave his own answer: "Because Buddhism presents itself as a way, a way of life, a journey, and Christianity has become a philosophy. An idea."[3]

It's hard to follow an idea. It's hard to walk in it. An idea you can argue and defend and slice up and promulgate (*promulgate*: a word so wooden anyone would only ever use it in connection with an idea). But it's hard to embody one. You can analyze an idea, but you can't walk in it.

I think I understood that Christianity is the Way when I first came to faith. Even more, I understood that Jesus is the Way. Later, I forgot all this and had to come back to it. But my first encounter with Christianity was actually an encounter with Jesus. I heard his "Come, follow me" almost audibly, certainly viscerally, and took him literally. Like his first disciples, I left what I was doing and followed him. My walking was inseparable from my believing. Indeed, my walking was the outward expression of my believing. I was a follower of Jesus. I experienced this—again, in ways I later forgot and had to recover—as a daily invitation, actually as a series of daily invitations, some large and dramatic, most small and mundane, to go in this direction rather than that one: peace rather than anger, honesty rather than duplicity, kindness rather than sarcasm, trust rather than fear. My days were marked by a thousand little forks in the road. I visualized it exactly like this: I could go this way or that. I could go the way I knew well and traveled often and knew where it led and never liked when I got there. Or I could go the way I didn't yet know and had not yet traveled and that went somewhere I hadn't yet imagined but which, I was learning, I would like very much. The first way almost always started out wide and easy, the other narrow and hard.

Anger, wide and easy. Peace, narrow and hard.

Lust, wide and easy. Love, narrow and hard.

Complaint, wide and easy. Thankfulness, narrow and hard.

Jesus never, not once, stood at the entrance of the wide and easy way beckoning me to follow. Always, he stood where the narrow way began, the hard and steep way. *This is the way,* he said. The more I went with him, the more I learned (and am still learning) to trust him, even though I can't think of even once when he showed me the end from the beginning.

Then I forgot all this. I started learning theology and doctrine and creeds and church distinctives and suchlike. All very good things. But they were never meant to replace the Way. But for me, they did. It was as if I started studying maps rather than walking the land the maps charted. I became something of an armchair connoisseur of maps. I could debate maps with other map experts. These debates sometimes got strenuous, heated, loud. They involved arguments about how to shade the maps, where to draw borderlines, what to name territories. It was all very engaging.

I walked less and less. I talked. I argued. I held opinions. But my legs, these grew rickety from disuse. Ideas took hold of me. The Way slipped away.

HOW TO BE A PASTOR

Then I became a pastor, which surprised many people, not the least myself, and most of all my wife. When I told her that a church, out of the blue, had contacted me to be their associate pastor, she said, "You can't be a pastor. Pastors are holy people."

That was a problem, for sure. But I needed work, and we needed money, and becoming a pastor was the only live option. My motive wasn't any more noble than that. So we packed up, moved to a small town, and I, a mere eight years after coming to faith, became a pastor. And my wife, not much holier than I, became a pastor's wife.

Neither of us had hardly a notion of what was involved. We hadn't grown up in church. We had no role models. I'd never even sat on a church committee prior to this. I was still naive enough to think that church boards wanted nothing so badly as to see the kingdom of God come in power and to pour themselves out like drink offerings to make it so.

Well, what happened is a long story. But I ended up a pastor in that church for more than six years, and then a pastor in another church for almost eighteen. I loved every day of it, except for the days I didn't. I loved every person in it, except for the people I didn't. All the leaders were just as I imagined, except the ones who weren't. But altogether, those were twenty-four amazing and difficult years, pretty much in equal measure, often intertwined.

I say all that to say this: to be a pastor, I had to learn to walk again. I had to return to the basic idea that discipleship is first and most about following Jesus. It's about walking with him, at God speed. Yes, I had to gain knowledge and skill, more than I had, in those things people expect from pastors—theological

27

soundness, biblical faithfulness, ethical uprightness. I had to become nicer and firmer both. I had to learn to preach and to give helpful counsel and to lead without bullying or cowering and to have some ideas about church music. I had to learn to perform weddings and funerals and to preside at the table. So many things to learn. I had to figure out that longwindedness and the wind of the Spirit rarely coincide—they tend to blow in opposite directions. I had to adjust, on the fly, from leaving one meeting where we hotly debated how many angels could dance on a pinhead to going to the next, where we had to decide what to do about a massive deficit that meant either the mortgage got paid or the payroll was met, just not both, to the next, where a woman had just discovered her husband's multiple infidelities and was caught between thoughts of murder and thoughts of suicide. It required more smarts, stamina, and integrity than I had.

Soon, and very soon, I found out that everything depended on walking, at God speed. Unless I was following Jesus, and walking with him, I had nothing to give and nothing to show. Unless I walked with Jesus, I was all talk. Another way of saying all this is that I got desperate again. I discovered, quickly, that I wasn't bright enough or good enough or gifted enough to be a pastor all on my lonesome. I wasn't, as Cheryl keenly observed, holy enough on my own.

I got in the habit of walking in the early morning before I preached. These were modest walks, usually two or three miles, rain or shine. I used the time to get my sermon in my bones, or at least in my belly. But more and more, I simply walked with Jesus. I talked with him about the sermon. He'd tell me things to say that I hadn't yet thought of and ways to say the things I had. Very often, these walks were emotional: Jesus made personal the passage I was about to preach. Often, I wept. The weeping was sometimes joyful and sometimes painful, depending. It was repentance sometimes, rejoicing at others, usually both.

At first, this walking was solely about my need. But I started to glimpse something else: it was good for the church. Walking set the Word down in me deeply. When I stepped into the pulpit, I spoke from a place of encounter. Every sermon—well, most anyhow—was not just an exposition but a testimony. It was bearing witness to a reality I had tasted and seen. With the apostle John, I could say, "That . . . which we have heard, which we have seen with our eyes, which we have looked at and our hands have touched—this we proclaim" (1 John 1:1).

Those walks changed me. And—I like to think, anyhow—they changed some of those to whom I spoke. At least a few people must have had a vague sense that behind what I said was something I had actually heard. What I shouted from the rooftop—or the pulpit—was a word Jesus had whispered in my ear. If I spoke with any authority at all, it was because of that, because the speaking grew from the listening, the conversation, the encounter.

If I talked well, it was because I walked first.

And more and more, I walked for no other reason than to keep company with Jesus. At least a few people must have had a vague sense that behind who I was, or was becoming, was someone I actually knew and walked with.

I am not a pastor anymore, not officially. But I still preach a lot. Often before I preach, I still walk. Billy Graham used to say about Cliff Barrows, the singer who accompanied him on most of his crusades, "I preach better after Cliff sings."

I preach better after I walk.

But for sure, I am better because I walk.

God Speed

JESUS CAME AND JESUS WENT

To learn how to walk in a spiritual sense, we have no better model than Jesus. So to learn from him, I go back, as is my bent, to the gospel of Mark. There, Jesus walks and walks. The few times he sits down or lays down, we're a bit shocked. It's in Matthew's and Luke's gospels that Jesus says, "Foxes have dens and birds have nests, but the Son of Man has no place to lay his head" (Matt. 8:20 and Luke 9:58), but it's Mark who provides the documentary evidence: *Jesus came* and *Jesus went* are among Mark's favorite phrases, often paired with *immediately*.

The one time we see Jesus sleeping—the only time in all the gospels—is on a boat that his disciples navigate. He falls asleep, it seems, because for once he's not walking. There he is, curled up among the tackle. I picture him, catlike, circling three times the spot he's about to bed down, testing the place for softness, folding himself into it. And he's out, dead asleep, deep dreaming amid surging waters, howling winds, bellowing fishermen. The disciples soon wake him anyhow—though four of them are seasoned seafarers, they've run out of options for keeping right side up in a tempest (Mark 4:35–38).

The next time the disciples cross that lake in a boat, Jesus walks on water through a crashing storm rather than ride with them (Mark 6:45–52)—certainly, a miraculous display of divine power and authority over the elements, natural and spiritual, but also maybe a sly comment about how pedestrian he is, how much he prefers walking to every other mode of getting around (and maybe an even slyer comment about how, once in a while, he needed a break from those men he traveled with, whose arguments and bickering and rivalries and goofy questions wore him down).

The few times we see Jesus sit—to teach, to eat, to hang out—there's a sense that he's both exhausted from all that walking and yet itching to get on with the next leg of the journey.

A car, a train, a bus, a small single-prop airplane—these weren't options. A caravan, yes, or a donkey, maybe. But Jesus eschewed these for reasons we don't know but can likely guess: he was keeping pace with the three-mile-an-hour God, going God speed. He needed the time to shape, slowly, slowly, the lives of those with whom he walked.

The Son of Man—the Human One, as one translation has it—is afoot. The perfect man, the man who represents our humanity, the man who is our brother, our spokesman, our effigy, our exemplar, our peace, our promise: that man walks and walks. And all along the way he invites us to follow him and, in the following, to become like him.

We know that following him is not literal anymore.

But does it still involve walking?

The apostle Peter suggests as much. When he meets, through an odd series of events, a Roman centurion named Cornelius in the city of Caesarea, he sums up the whole mission of Jesus in one rolling phrase that occupies no more than a single verse of Scripture. Here it is: "God anointed Jesus of

Nazareth with the Holy Spirit and power, and . . . he went around doing good and healing all who were under the power of the devil, because God was with him" (Acts 10:38).

And he went around doing good.

On your walk today, consider this question: what good can I do?

"As the Father has sent me," Jesus says, "I am sending you" (John 20:21). Our whole life, from here to there, is to keep filling to overflowing with the Holy Spirit. And then to walk a lot, doing good.

CHAPTER 3

A Brief History of Walking

Rebecca Solnit wrote a gorgeous and sprawling book in 2000 called *Wanderlust: A History of Walking*. It was a bestseller, which typically doesn't happen to books with the word *history* in the title—or (and this is my great fear) to books with *walking* in the title, either. She doesn't attempt a systematic treatment of pedestrianism—hers is a quirky, lopsided, shambling account of walks and walkers, laced with philosophical musings, and all stitched together with stories of her wanderings. But she does cover a lot of ground (pun intended) and says much about the history of walking.

I commend her book to you, partly because it's a good read and partly because the title of this chapter is a flat-out lie: I have no intention—and, frankly, lack sufficient knowledge—to provide herein a history of walking. Go to Solnit for that.

But I exaggerate: my chapter title is not exactly a lie. It's just a case of overpromising. What I do intend here is a whirlwind survey of walking, from the first archeological evidence for it to the modern march to justice.

WHY TWO LEGS?

In 1976, in Laetoli, Tanzania, Africa, Mary Leakey and her team of paleontologists *stumbled*—that's the word the Smithsonian uses—upon animal tracks that, two years later, led to the discovery of two pairs of hominin footprints, fossilized in volcanic ash. The footprints mark a brief segment of a journey of two (or perhaps three) people striding. The hardened ash dates to 3.6 million years ago, making these footprints the oldest evidence we have for bipedalism—walking on two limbs, not four.[4]

The footprints are not of equal size or span. One of the walkers is much smaller than the other and lags behind. She is hurrying to keep up.

Where have they been? Where are they going? Why are they out and afoot? Is it a mother and her child, fleeing a terrible man? Have they been gathering brushwood or berries, things needed for survival, and now are bundling them back to their shelter? Are they visiting a relative? A friend? Are they seeking something beyond themselves, bigger than themselves, someone to thank, to seek consolation from, maybe to worship?

All we know is they walked.

But why were they walking at all? Why were they on two legs, rather than four? There's no apparent advantage to bipedalism.[5] A creature on two legs is not faster than a creature on four. If it's speed you want, it goes in the opposite direction: think cheetah or wolf or even elephant—all outrun a human, no matter how fast and agile that human is. A hippopotamus can outpace an Olympic sprinter. And if it's stability you seek, standing on two legs is a bad idea. Anything, animate or inanimate, is ricketier on two limbs than on four, more prone to tip over or, if moving, to stumble.

No, there's no clear advantage to walking on two legs. Evolutionary scientists have vigorous, sometimes vicious, debates about why we started doing it in the first place—why anyone stood upright and stayed that way. Was it to lessen the intensity of the hot sun beating down on our backs? Was it to show off and parade around our reproductive equipment to attract a mate, because we lack plumes and tail feathers, or horns and tusks, or beautiful throaty warbly songs that might help with that? Was it to stretch ourselves skyward and make ourselves look bigger to scare off our enemies, to compensate for our otherwise unimpressive physical dimensions?

Or was this just how God made us?

Well, maybe the point is moot. Here we are, all standing tall-ish. After infancy, only spelunking or playing children's games or navigating steep treacherous terrain or managing certain kinds of injuries or looking for lost things under low things puts us back on all fours. Otherwise, we all stride about swinging one leg after the other, back and forth. We're all two-stepping.

It costs us. We get hunched shoulders. We get sore backs. We get blistered toes. We get creaky knees. We get aching hips. Walking is not, it turns out, the best way to care for your body. And yet we don't resort, except under usually forced conditions, to anything else. For most of our history, before we domesticated horses, before we invented powered ways of travel, walking was the only way to get anywhere on hard ground.

You need to find water? You want to discover where the bison go when they go away or where egrets fly when they pick up, en masse, and blur the air with their disappearing? You must walk.

And even after humans found other ways to get around, all of us still—all the time, everywhere—can go only so far before we must walk. Every day, most of us navigate some part of the world on our legs. It's simple necessity.

ON THE MOVE

Of course, beyond necessity, many of us also *choose* to walk. Strolls. Hikes. Jaunts. Pilgrimages. Not all of our walking is obligatory. In this past year I've spoken to people who walked, by choice, and in some cases at great expense, a section of the coast of Wales, a holy trail through rural northeast England, a chunk of Spain's El Camino de Santiago, a mountain in China, a mountain in Guatemala, a trail through the Navajo desert, another through the Adirondacks. No one made them do this. All of them paid to do this. Most of them suffered from doing this—from sore calves and bone-weariness, if nothing else, but also from lost wages, sprains and injuries and food poisoning and, in one case, a broken bone and bee stings. Yet all said that the walk was a highlight of their year, in some cases their lives.

This impulse has a deep root. People have been on the move from way back. Most of this was pure necessity: tracking elk herds, chasing sunlight, avoiding enemies, finding fresh water supplies, seeking fertile valleys. Wars and famines and climate change and animal migrations or extinctions—all explains most human movement for much of the time we've been here. With our world's ongoing and increasing refugee crises, it doesn't look like humanity's moving about will slow down anytime soon.

Some were forced to walk because of banishment. The first forced walker in Scripture was Cain, whom God cursed to be a restless wanderer for killing his brother. He didn't walk far. Next thing, he's building a city—which, come to think of it, is almost by definition a locus of restless wanderers.

But in general, humans are more migratory than sedentary. We've spent most of our existence zipping about the planet. We're all restless wanderers. Staying put is the exception.

Most of this walking we did because we had little or no choice.

But not always.

Some people have walked because they just plain wanted to and because they could and because they were curious and because they fell under the spell of wanderlust. They walked because they had more aliveness in their limbs than hunting mastodon and harvesting wild berries could exhaust. They walked because they grew bored and looked at a horizon and thought, *I wonder what's on the other side of that?*

We all have a nesting impulse, a longing for deep roots. But it competes, sometimes goes to war, with a drive to strike out in new directions, to go tramping, even wildfaring. For example, here I sit in a plush leather chair beside a warm fire, a cup of dark-roast coffee on my armrest, the only sound my breath and the clack of my fingers on the keyboard. I am safe and comfortable, and stationary. But sometimes I dream of cold lands and deep shadows and a north wind bearing down smelling of snow, and fresh tracks in the wet earth, huge, topped with curves and holes that only the claws of a large and dangerous animal could make.

I'm guessing most of us, to varying degrees, feel these two impulses too. One part of us seeks a life to which our main response is a sigh of contentment, a yawn of boredom. Another part seeks a different life, very different, to which our main response is a whoop of daring, a howl of terror.

A part of us wants to just sit here, and the other to strike out on a journey. All of this is part of our history, all the way back.

CHRISTIAN PILGRIMAGE

Christians have made their contribution to the history of walking. The tradition of pilgrimage arose in Christian Europe in the fourth century (although there are hints of it prior to that). It was originally and exclusively connected with visiting the Holy Land. This eventually produced a flourishing commerce in wayfarer's inns and guide services and a brisk trade in relics.[6] In time, other sites besides the Holy Land became pilgrimage destinations—for Catholics, sites such as Santiago de Compostela in Spain or Lourdes in France; for Protestants, places such as St. Davids Cathedral in Wales or the shrine of St. Thomas Becket in Canterbury.[7]

The Christian tradition is captured, most famously, in the eighteenth-century pious allegory *Pilgrim's Progress*, John Bunyan's chronicle of an everyman, Christian, as he wends his way to the Celestial City. It is a tale of learning steadfast faith and virtue in the face of many trials, seductions, and distractions. I have a whole chapter about it later.

The tradition of pilgrimage is also captured in less-pious literature, the most famous of which is Chaucer's *The Canterbury Tales*, a rollicking and often bawdy epic poem recounting the wayfaring and storytelling of several pilgrims as they plod their way from London to the shrine of Thomas Becket in Canterbury. The whole purpose of the trip is to win a contest for the best story. The winner gets a free dinner at the Tabard Inn in Southwark.

The Canterbury Tales is uproarious reading. But it also is an unwitting testament to how much the idea of Christian pilgrimage corroded in a thousand or so years, from its beginnings to Chaucer's time.

For centuries, the deep drive beneath Christian pilgrimage was penance: one traveled as a form of travail. You walked to suffer. You undertook privation and hardship for sins committed and virtues neglected. You walked to make amends, to somehow, step by weary step, undo your wrongdoing. You went footsore and hungry in order to return chastened, humbled, restored. You bent low to come back upright.

Other motives also drove pilgrimage: the need for a fresh start, the quest for a vision, the discernment of one's future, the consecration of oneself. Above all, a pilgrim sought God. A pilgrim traveled to a place where God had moved and spoken in times past, in the hope that God would move and speak now. A pilgrim journeyed to see and to touch things that bore witness to heaven meeting earth, in the hope that heaven would do it again.

Pope Benedict XVI put it this way: "To go on pilgrimage is not simply to visit a place to admire its treasures of nature, art or history. To go on pilgrimage really means to step out of ourselves in order to encounter God where he has revealed himself, where his grace has shone with particular splendour and produced rich fruits of conversion and holiness among those who believe."[8]

Over time, the tradition of pilgrimage weakened and now is virtually nonexistent. Not that people don't still go on pilgrimages. They do, and in increasing numbers. Indeed, walking ancient pilgrimage trails has become something of a rage. Only, few go anymore with religious motivation. Few walk as an act of penance or to seek an encounter with heaven. For the most part, something else now calls people, drives them, sustains them.

What replaced pilgrimage are treks, walkathons, and public marches.

TREKS, WALKATHONS, AND MARCHES

Consider, for a moment, treks. I have been reading, as part of my research for this book, Sarah Baxter's delightful *A History of the World in 500 Walks*. She documents, sometimes in no more than a dozen words, sometimes in lengthy text combined with maps and tips and travel routes and color photos, five hundred walks on all seven continents. She takes us from red-sand deserts to craggy mountain passes, from rain forest cocoons to stark tundra expanses, through land impossibly ancient, past artifacts impressively old. She takes us to historical cradles and turning points, where revolutions began, where founding documents were signed, where battles raged, where movements, sometimes whole nations, were birthed or shattered. Some of these walks you can do in a day, even a few hours. Most take a week or two. Some take months, some the better part of a year.

Baxter often warns about the various hazards of each walk: this route's grueling arduousness, this one's inclement weather, this one's large population of venomous snakes or hungry predators or pesky bugs. In former times, most of us would con-template such a trip on foot only if we had a compelling goal, such as sheer necessity, or for religious reasons. We needed to find food or escape an invader or work something out, shake something off, or find God or forgiveness.

Now people do this for fun. They do it for the thrill or maybe to snap a selfie by some legendary shrine and thereby secure bragging rights. Not that some of the discoveries that birthed and propelled pilgrimage don't still happen, especially on longer quests. We still walk to find things, avoid things, work things out, shake things off, find God, find forgiveness. I think about Cheryl Strayed's story *Wild*, in which she grieved the death of her mother and overcame her patterns of self-destruction by walking, alone, with naively inadequate preparation, the Pacific Crest Trail, some 1,100 miles of it. Or Robyn Davidson, who walked, again alone except for a dog, almost the entire continent of Australia, 1,700 miles from Alice Springs to the Indian Ocean, and came to some peace with her past. Neither woman began her journey with a clear sense of why. Treks, it turns out, can turn into pilgrimages. Transformation is sometimes a by-product of a walk begun for different reasons or no reason at all.

In general, pilgrimages have become treks.

But they've also become walkathons. This walking is like a pilgrimage in that it's undertaken with a goal in mind and is done, as many though not all pilgrimages are done, in the company of others. But it's unlike pilgrimage in that, depending on the goal, it is usually more of a festive thing than a purgative one. People walk to raise money for a cause. They walk to raise awareness about an issue. They walk to show solidarity around a concern. But altogether, they walk to do good, maybe to feel good, maybe to change things, but not to change themselves or see the face of God.

There's also the march, the collective walk. Like a pilgrimage, it is goal oriented and communal. Often it has a kind of shrine or sacred site in view—a seat of government, a cultural icon, a historical location. It's the Mall in Washington, DC. It's Parliament in Ottawa. It's Tiananmen Square in Beijing, or Red Square in Moscow.

Marchers in a march are after something. Justice. Peace. Freedom. Impeachment. Revolution. Clean water. The end of discrimination. Accountable government. The end of war. The march is about change, just like a pilgrimage. But unlike a pilgrimage, the change sought is always *out there*, not in here. It's about others changing, but not me.

Which is not to say marches are wrong. Many marches have done great good. Some have changed society and history. Some are David and Goliath tales: a terrible menace or injustice, seemingly invincible, felled by the single stone of a crowd on their feet.

But their weakness, to say it again, is that marches always target the problem *out there*. Sure enough, the problem is out there. But it's also *in here*. It's them, and it's us. It's me. This is why many marches, even when they accomplish great things, often have no lasting impact: because people who march need to be the recipients of change, not just agents of it.

Which is something pilgrimages were good at.

God Speed

WALKING IN UNITY

Some marches are not against anyone or anything. They are marches for something or someone. Jesus. Peace. Hope. Unity.

In a town where I lived for many years, a few of us organized an annual Walk of the Nations. It wasn't against anything. It was a sign of unity. We called upon the community—schools, churches, business, government, First Nations leaders, clubs, and all and any individuals—to walk together. Hundreds responded. We walked together as a sign that, whatever the differences between us, we were neighbors. We all loved our children and our parents. We all wanted a community that was safe and flourishing. We all wanted to live without fear, hunger, hate. So we walked. As far as I know, that community still gathers every year to do this.

This kind of walking—walking as a sign of unity—has a deep echo in the twenty-five Psalms, from 120 to 134, called the Songs of Ascents. These songs were sung by pilgrims making their way to Jerusalem, to the temple, to gather and to worship and to feast. It was a march of sorts. But it was a march *for* something, to do something: to worship, to celebrate, to give thanks.

The beauty of this kind of walking is that it levels all social classes. Rich and poor, old and young, male and female, slave and free, every tribe and tongue and nation—all walk together to the same place and sing as they go. The singing, as the walking, helps level differences. It declares shared cause and shared faith and shared humanity.

I wonder what it would look like to recover something of this in our churches. In liturgical churches, a form of the Ascent Psalms is preserved in processionals, where the community sings as the officiants march into the sanctuary, holding the Scriptures aloft.

I dream of being part of a church that does this. We walk together singing. We invite onlookers to join us. I think it would be as much an embodiment of and invitation to the gospel as any overt act of evangelism. Who wouldn't want to go to a church where we sang our way getting there?

For your next walk, consider inviting along two or three fellow church members. Find something that will unify you—a cause, a prayer, a penitence, or a praise—and enact your oneness in a walk.

CHAPTER 4

Walk This Way

Whether you turn to the right or to the left,
your ears will hear a voice behind you, saying,
"This is the way; walk in it."

—ISAIAH 30:21

*This is what the L*ORD *says:*

"Stand at the crossroads and look;
*   ask for the ancient paths,*
ask where the good way is, and walk in it,
*   and you will find rest for your souls.*
*   But you said, 'We will not walk in it.'"*

—JEREMIAH 6:16

O ne of these passages is good news, the other not. Isaiah is
doing what Isaiah often does—promising God's abundant
grace despite Israel's cussed waywardness. And Jeremiah, he's
doing what he mostly does—lamenting Israel's cussed waywardness despite God's abundant grace. Isaiah drips promise and
Jeremiah bristles indictment. Most of us—or me, anyhow—need
a heavy and regular dose of both.

But the common ground between these two prophets is the
call to walk "in the way"—the good way, *this* way. Implying that
there is also a bad way. A *not this* way. Which makes perfect
sense. Not all roads lead to a destination worth arriving at. Only,
this is seldom obvious at the start of any road. As Proverbs says,
and Jesus does too, a road that looks inviting in the first few
miles, or even the first few thousand, might turn treacherous.
Contrariwise, a road that looks menacing or unpromising at the
get-go might lead, given enough distance, to a place lush and
light soaked (e.g., Prov. 2:12–15; 7:24–27; Matt. 7:13–14).

Neither Isaiah nor Jeremiah says exactly what or where the
good way is. Isaiah says we need intimate, almost moment-by-
moment, maybe-supernatural guidance to find it. Jeremiah says
we need to stand and look and ask in order to find it. Probably
it's both—some rigorous inquiry matched with some timely and
sometimes otherworldly prompting.

Jeremiah says these good roads are ancient. They've been
around a while. They're well known, or at least once were: likely,
most are now overgrown, largely forgotten, bypassed. Isaiah says
we usually know the path and stay on it only by heeding a voice,
a voice right behind us, a voice whispering to us. We discover the
ancient path by searching. And we walk that path by listening.

We need a map or a marked trail.

And we need a guide.

But the way is so old, so ancient, most people have forgotten it ever existed. It's not clear cut anymore. It's not waymarked, and maps are rare. You have to stand at a crossroad—where the landscape opens out—and look for it, hard. You have to ask around, probably among the old-timers, some of whom will barely recollect where it is, where it goes, how long it stretches. And then, most of all, you've got to set out. It's not a path that can be known except by walking. Some others, once you ask them, will have tales to tell of their own journeys, but these secondhand accounts are no substitute for making the journey yourself. The way, Antonio Machado said, is made by walking.

What does such asking involve? Jeremiah suggests it's literal—you inquire among those well traveled, among the knowledge keepers. You ask them which is the best route from where you are now to where you need to go. The good way is not necessarily the quickest way or the easiest or even the safest. Its goodness is that it gets you there and does its work in you as you go. And when you ask, it's not only geographical information you seek. You want lore, tales, wisdom: "In the first small village you come to, you will see an inn whose beauty and music will tempt you to enter and stay. Avoid it. The man who runs it is a crook, and you will wake with a sore head and a light purse. Instead, half a mile farther on is a rustic hostel with a low roof. Its homeliness will tempt you to pass by. Don't. The widow who owns it is honest and kind and the best cook in the land. Leave her a good tip."

Jeremiah's poetic language suggests that the ancient paths are not merely, or even mainly, terrestrial: they are also, perhaps mostly, spiritual. He means by "paths" ways of knowing, of living, of being. There is the way of kindness. The way of generosity. The way of boldness. The way of peace. The way of humility.

All these are good and ancient ways. All have been known, forgotten, rediscovered, forgotten again. All are only known, known truly and fully, by walking. They are good because, hard as they often are, they call us step by step to deeper goodness and form us step by step in that goodness.

Often our motivation for looking and asking for a good way comes from walking in a bad way—the way of meanness or greed or pride or cowardice or violence. Walking in a bad way always leads to a reckoning: we act out our violent temper in a traffic incident, or our greed leads to theft, or our cowardice to lying, or our pain to addiction. And maybe then we realize, *I can't do this anymore. I can't keep traveling this way any farther. I don't know exactly what lies at the end of this road, but I know I don't want to find out.*

It's then we stand at a crossroads. It's then we look, look hard. It's then we ask, "Is there a different road? Is there a good way?"

FIND THE GOOD WAY

My main practice of looking and asking and finding and walking ancient paths and good ways has been to cultivate a life in Scripture. I spent my first twenty-one years without once cracking open a Bible. When my brother, who recently had come to faith, gave me a Bible for Christmas—I think it was 1980, when I was twenty—I let it sit unopened for six or seven months. I thought it was a waste of a gift, and an insult to boot. He could have bought me a case of beer. He could have bought me tickets to a Queen concert. He could have given me cash and let me pick my gift. Even, he could have got me socks or underwear and at least I would have made use of them. But he got me a Bible, which I had no intention of reading and which implied that my life was weighed in the balance and found wanting. That I lacked something.

Which, indeed, I did. I was both stuck and careening—going nowhere but out of control. Every step took me closer to somewhere I didn't want to be, to becoming someone I didn't want to become. So one day, bored as much as curious, I picked up the book. I read Genesis quickly. It was wondrous and strange. I started into Exodus and soon stalled. I called my mother—I didn't want to confess to my brother that I had started the book he gave me—and told her that the book was boring and confusing. She also had recently come to faith. She told me that I wasn't to read the Bible like a normal book, front to back, start to finish, but to jump around in it. I should start, she said, in the Gospels and then Acts and then the Epistles and then maybe the Psalms and Proverbs. She had to explain what all this meant.

I glanced through the Gospels. I discovered that one was named after me, or vice versa. The gospel named after me, or vice versa, was the shortest of the four. I cottoned on to it for that reason.

What I didn't know until later is that I stood at a crossroads, looking, asking. Seeking a good way, an ancient way, a new way.

What I did find, startlingly, is Jesus leaping off the pages. Jesus blazing out of nowhere, with dazzling suddenness, without even a greeting, rearranging everything, upending everyone's lives.

The heavens tear open.

The Spirit descends.

The Father speaks.

Then the Spirit drives Jesus headlong into the desert. Satan and angels and wild animals all crowd into a single sentence, maybe a single scene. Then Jesus speaks. He announces and commands. He tells tradesmen to leave their jobs and families. *You, you, you, you.* A demon-possessed man hears him speak, flips out, bellows and thrashes, and Jesus shuts him right up. Sick people hunt Jesus down, beg him for just a touch, and he heals them.

And that's just the first chapter, and not even all of it.

About a third of the way through Mark, I came to a tentative conclusion: Jesus was either plum crazy or the most interesting person who ever lived. I had to find out which. I decided to follow him, which isn't the same thing as believing in him. I was just going to tag along for a stretch, see where things got.

I kept reading. Standing at the crossroads. Looking. Asking. Following. Walking.

Jesus enraged me, delighted me, inspired me, troubled me, and always and in every way intrigued me. I would read some portion—his rudeness, for instance, to people who asked him the same questions I wanted to ask him—and think, *Ah, I guess he's not the one for me.* But then I'd read something else—how Jesus dealt with a sick woman or told stories or cared for people whom others despised—and I'd think, *Well, maybe I'll go a few more miles, see how I'm feeling then.*

After a long time, I decided that, though likely some things about Jesus would always perplex me and trouble me, he was worth my whole attention and, yes, obedience—which meant, then and now, if he told me to do something, I'd do it regardless of whether I was inclined toward it or even understood it. I decided to follow him always, everywhere.

I chose to believe in him. The Jesus who turns the world upside down turned my world upside down.

I still sometimes lose my way. I still sometimes walk in a bad way. But every time I do, I go back to the book and the one whom the book points to. I stand at the crossroads. I look. I ask. And I find, fresh as though I stumbled on it just then, the ancient paths. I find the Ancient of Days. The good ways. The Good Way.

And I walk.

FIND A GUIDE

Jeremiah tells us to find a way.

Isaiah tells us to heed a guide. "Whether you turn to the right or to the left, your ears will hear a voice behind you, saying, 'This is the way; walk in it.'"

I'm cheap. So when I'm visiting some place of interest—a museum or art gallery or historic site where a decisive battle was fought or a queen crowned or an important document signed and such—I usually self-guide. There's almost always a map that comes with admission, and interpretive signs all around. I use these. They seem enough. Later, I tell people that I toured such and such a place and how fascinating it was and that I saw, say, some really cool swords. But if anyone presses me for details, I quickly draw a blank.

Then one day, someone I was with hired a guide. Oh my. That made all the difference in the world. I didn't need the map. I ignored the interpretive signs. The guide knew all that stuff, and then some. Even more, the guide knew how to connect everything: the battle with the crowning with the signing with the metallurgy behind the swords.

Since then, I often hire a guide. I've learned that a good guide is not only knowledgeable, she's also wise. She has more than memorized a script. She's lived deeply into the story. She knows what happened, yes, but also what it means, how the past reaches into the present. It's in her bones. She's made the old story her own.

This is the difference between having a map and having a guide. The best map won't tell you which way to go. The best interpretive signs still won't help you find your way. A map is good, but a guide is gold.

That's what Isaiah seems to be saying: use the map, sure, but also heed the guide.

Is he talking about the Holy Spirit? That intimate companion who never leaves our side and leads us into all truth? The comforter and advocate who gives us strength along the way? The guide who brings more than knowledge, who also imparts wisdom and connects everything to everything?

That's how it is for me, increasingly. My pressing need when I first started reading the Bible at twenty-one was to know what it says. But I've soaked in Scripture now for nearly forty years and learned much of it. There are still big gaps in my knowing. But the big stuff I largely have. Who is God that I should obey him? What has God given to me? What does God require of me? Is it right to pay taxes to Caesar? Am I my brother's keeper? How many times should I forgive a brother who sins against me?

All this and more I know.

But often now it's guidance I need, not knowledge. What

I lack is not information but discernment. The map—that I've almost committed to memory. But navigating the terrain? That only a guide can give.

I don't always know, for instance, what obedience looks like in the gray zones, in situations where there is no clear right or wrong. I don't always know, for instance, the limits of my political allegiance—when Revelation 13's call to resist Caesar takes precedence over Romans 13's call to submit to him. That requires discernment. I can't always figure out the difference between the grace that opens up fresh possibility and makes room for genuine change, and the grace that merely perpetuates abuse and keeps letting the abuser walk away unchanged. That requires discernment. I don't always know when caring for another person is sheer selfless compassion and when it is only enablement or codependence or false altruism. That requires discernment.

For such things, I don't need another Bible verse. I do need, and seek, wise and prayerful counsel. But especially, I need the Holy Spirit. A voice behind me whispering in my ear—that close, that intimate—saying, "This is the way; walk in it."

It happened recently. My wife and I were very serious about buying a piece of property to house and expand some of the ministry we do. We found the perfect property. We met with the owners and told them our vision. They were excited. We were excited. We gathered, on the property, some of the people who have been our wise and prayerful counselors over many years. They were excited. We were excited. We sensed that this was the right time and the right place. We went home to set everything in motion.

Then I heard a voice, right behind me. The voice said, *Wait*.

The voice said it was not the time and not the place. The voice said to go back to the owners and tell them. I told my wife. She had heard the voice too.

As I write this, almost a year has gone by since that moment. The owners have sold the property to another buyer. We have not found another piece of land. We are both disappointed and comforted. We trust that the voice has led us well and will again.

There is, as I have said, no Scripture that gives guidance this specific, this explicit, this immediate. More knowledge wouldn't have made the difference. Only guidance. Only a voice, right behind us, telling us where to walk and where not to.

Scripture gives direction. It makes ancient ways new. The Holy Spirit gives guidance. He makes the ancient ways personal.

It's a potent combination.

Walk this way.

God Speed

RETRACING YOUR STEPS

The usual way to find something you've lost—your hat, your phone, your wallet, your water bottle—is to retrace your steps: think about where you've been and walk it in reverse. I've done this many times. Once—okay, twice—I left a bag in the security area of a major airport. Another time, I left my passport in a store. More times than I can count I've left my keys or sunglasses somewhere—a restaurant table, the ledge of a public bathroom, the hood of the car. Now that I'm writing all this down, I realize I have a knack for losing things. Each time—unless I have sudden searing recall of exactly where I've left the thing—I retrace my steps. Only a few times have I failed to recover the lost item.

This is also a good way to recover other lost things: hope, faith, love, courage, kindness. Your heart. The way to find your way back to the Way is this: just retrace your steps.

The Prodigal Son did that (Luke 15:11–32). He ran away, far away, and soon ran out of money. He lost a lot: his passport, his father's Amex, his airport lounge passes, the keys to the Porsche. Then his food vouchers. His good complexion. His so-called friends. His dignity.

But mostly, he lost himself. He forgot who he was, and whose.

One day in a fit of hunger he woke up. He came to his senses, is how Luke describes it, which is funny, because all the while we thought he was indulging them. He started to feel things again. Sadness. Shame. Real desire. The memory of joy. The goodness of bread. And he got up and retraced his steps. He walked all the way home. And all the way, he rehearsed an apology: *I have sinned. I am not worthy. Make me one of your hired servants.* His father, it turns out, would have none of it. He had enough servants. What the father wanted—what he ran to reclaim—was his son.

That boy had to go backward before he could move forward. He had to retrace his steps.

I know a man who did this with his marriage. His affection for his wife had thinned to near invisibility. Her laughter that once delighted him now irritated him. Her body that once entranced him now bored him. Her clumsiness used to charm him but now frustrated him. He began dreaming about being alone or being with someone else.

But he retraced his steps. He had traveled a long way to get to this place of irritation, frustration, boredom. It spanned many years, traversed a thousand complicated routes. He went back all the way to the day they met. He saw her as an eighteen-year-old—her mix of confidence and shyness, the way she shrugged her shoulders and laughed at herself, her love for the elderly. Back then, he couldn't stop looking at her. When apart, he couldn't stop thinking about her. No one had ever stormed his world the way she did. No one had ever made him alive like she did. All he wanted was her.

He went all the way back and found what he lost, and recovered the thing whole.

I've done this a few times with lost things. Conviction. Hope. A sense of God's goodness or nearness. I wake up one day and realize I haven't seen or heard from this thing in quite a while. Where did I last see it? I retrace my steps. I return along the route I've come until I get back to that place where, as the writer of Hebrews says, I first came into the light (Heb. 10:32). To be clear, I'm not looking to recover a simplistic faith or naive enthusiasm or shallow piety, things that marked me out in earlier years. It's more what Paul describes in his letter to the Philippians: "I . . . take hold of that for which Christ Jesus took hold of me" (Phil. 3:12). I go looking for that. Most times, I recover the thing whole.

And more times than not, this recovery is done by walking. I retrace my steps by actually taking steps. I get air in my lungs. Wind on my face. Hard ground beneath my feet. Bright heaven above my head.

Is there anything you've lost along the way—joy or trust or boldness or humility or affection or generosity? Name it. Try to recall where you last saw it. Then walk backward until you find it.

Go, take a walk, and recover the thing whole.

CHAPTER 5

The Reason You Walk

Indigenous journalist, musician, activist, and now politician Wab Kinew's memoir, *The Reason You Walk*, became an instant bestseller in Canada when it was released in September 2015. Its immediate and wide popularity was partly because of a rapidly rising interest among Canadians in indigenous peoples and their cultures. In turn, that interest—for large swaths of our history, Canadians have mostly displayed ignorance about and indifference or fear toward First Nations people—was largely because of the findings, also released in 2015, of Canada's Truth and Reconciliation Commission (TRC), a six-year oral-history project that explored and exposed the history and legacy of Canada's Indian Residential Schools.[9] The TRC gathered the live testimonies of more than six thousand indigenous men and women who survived the often brutal conditions of these schools—separation from family, malnourishment, poor and haphazard education, and abuse at every level: verbal, emotional, physical, sexual, and spiritual.

Wab Kinew's father, Tobasonakwut, was a survivor of such a school in northern Ontario. He was forcibly removed from his family. He was shamed out of his culture and language. He was beaten. He was emotionally abused. He was sexually molested.

All of this harm damaged Tobasonakwut's capacities as a father. The early years of Wab's relationship with Tobasonakwut were marked by anger, strife, violence, estrangement, and deep hurt. But in 2012, Wab found out Tobasonakwut was dying from cancer. He committed that entire year to healing their relationship. The book mostly narrates that year. It is a beautiful and poignant story. As part of Tobasonakwut's journey, he embraces a form of Catholicism much kinder than what he was exposed to in residential school. And Wab finds hope and identity through his practice of the sundance.

The title of the book gives away its heart: the reason you walk is to work out your pain and identity. One reviewer of the book said it is "not just a memoir . . . [but] a meditation on the purpose of living."[10] You walk, Kinew says, to come to a place of healing, forgiveness, wholeness, reconciliation, peace. You walk to discover and step into your truest and deepest self, the real you. You walk to face your past, without bitterness, and to live in your present, without fear, and to move toward your future, with hope and courage. You walk to make your peace with God. "How wise our ancestors were," Kinew writes, "to leave us with this path to walk. . . . [S]omehow, when we walk this path as others did before ourselves, we get what we need. . . . To be hurt, yet forgive. To do wrong, but forgive yourself. To depart from this world leaving only love. This is the reason you walk."[11]

VISION QUEST

Underneath Wab's book title lies a deep tradition among many North American indigenous peoples: the vision quest. A vision quest draws heavily on tradition and legend, but it's also about finding one's place in the world and in the community. It's about identity. And it's about the present and the future.

The vision quest, traditionally, was a rite of passage for males. Undertaken around his fourteenth year, it marked a young man's transition from boyhood to manhood. It began typically with a four-day fast, in isolation. Then the boy walked into wilderness, without provisions, sometimes with a single weapon, sometimes without one.

Some non-native people and groups—and worse, businesses— have tried to replicate these quests. They are almost all caricatures, usually with comical,[12] though sometimes with tragic, results.[13]

What I am commending is something other than that—not a mimicry of a vision quest but a deep inquiry into the reason you walk. The vision quest was about discovering, personally, uniquely, deep down, your connection with the Creator, with the creation, with your people, with yourself. Indigenous peoples have, in various forms, ways of enacting that.

But the fundamental purpose underneath the vision quest— discovering, personally, uniquely, deep down, your connection with the Creator and the earth and your people and yourself— remains necessary work for all of us. As Wab Kinew discovered, unless he was willing to go on a journey of remembering and forgetting, of confessing and forgiving, of confronting and relinquishing, of healing his wounds and the wounds of others, he was not ever going to know himself, or anyone else, deeply and truly. He would play at the surface, masking or denying or indulging his pain, living a shadow self bent on a false quest.

The same is true of us: without a journey of remembering and forgetting, of confessing and forgiving, of confronting and relinquishing, of healing our wounds and the wounds of others, we will not ever know ourselves, or anyone else, deeply and truly.

So I am commending a vision quest of sorts.

A PEDESTRIAN PILGRIMAGE

It turns out Christians, historically, traditionally, have practiced a kind of vision quest of our own. It's called pilgrimage. When I first set out to write this book, I thought I was going to research and write largely on the history of pilgrimage and its current practices. I kept watching films—movies, some, documentaries, others—on the Camino de Santiago, sometimes simply called the Way, one of the oldest and certainly the most famous of Christian pilgrimage routes. The Way has experienced an over-whelming resurgence of popularity in the past few decades, largely because of said movies and documentaries.[14]

Obviously, I didn't write that book. It would have taken more time and money than I have, more travel and research than I'm up for. And besides, after I thought about it, I realized that pilgrimage is not the kind of walking I'm mostly interested in—lengthy treks that take weeks or months to complete and usually require extensive travel beforehand and afterward. Mostly, only well-off people can afford them. I was aiming for something more pedestrian. I agree with what Rebecca Solnit writes in *Wanderlust:* "The surprises, liberations, and clarifications of travel can sometimes be garnered by going around the block as well as going around the world."[15]

Trevor Herriot writes,

> When friends tell me they are going to Nepal to fill their creative well, or to Machu Picchu to do a prayer walk, my first response has always been a generous twinge of envy, but my second thought is, Can you restore your soul by taking it to places where it won't know the other souls? Where the way the creek turns, the quality of the sunlight, the conversation of the birds will all be unfamiliar? . . . Undoubtedly, one can have a profound religious experience on a trek that requires travel agents, a 747, and hotels, but when you are as cheap as I am, you claim the high road any way you can. I decided I would follow the simple pattern laid down by every spiritual seeker . . . : pack lightly, get my best walking sandals on, and head out the door. I had no desire to get any more religion than I already had, but I wanted to walk out into the country and place my questions before the humbler revelation written into a creek, a roadside lily, or a stand of Aspen.[16]

And so he walked out to the edge of the city he lived in. That's what I have in mind.

Also, a pilgrimage, as I note in chapter 3, has historically often had as much (or more) to do with penance as with finding oneself. A pilgrimage was about working out one's salvation with fear and trembling. (See Phil. 2:12.) Modern pilgrimages are almost all about the latter, about finding oneself, which I am interested in, but also wary of. I do think that some of our deepest and most important work is becoming clear about who we are. It's about identity. But I also think this quest has largely been hijacked in Western culture and is in danger of becoming self-indulgent, even narcissistic.

Anyhow, that's a long (and maybe self-indulgent and narcissistic) explanation for why I abandoned my original idea to write on pilgrimage.

But pilgrimage was one of the primary ways for many centuries that Christians, and not just wealthy ones, worked out their salvation with fear and trembling. As I said, much of this had a penitential quality to it: I had lived poorly and wronged others grievously and wandered perilously, and now this journey, long and arduous and involving suffering, sacrifice, and privation, was both the way I made things right and the way I learned obedience.

Some of this happens as a matter of course when we set out on pilgrimage. We don't engineer or manufacture it. We don't even go looking for it. It just falls out with our footfalls. It gathers with the miles.

The movie *The Way* is a good illustration of this, about a man who walks El Camino. It's a fictionalized story, but true to the experience of many who walk there now. In the movie, not one of the people whose stories it tells sets out with any religious motivation. The penitential element is absent. One man, Joost, wants to lose weight. A bitter woman, Sarah, wants to quit smoking. An Irish writer, Jack, wants a good story. The main character, Tommy (played by Martin Sheen), is grieving, sort of. His son Daniel (played by Sheen's real-life son, Emilio Estevez), from whom he has been estranged, dies walking El Camino. Tommy travels from the US to France to collect his son's ashes and belongings. But while there, he makes a spur-of-the-moment decision to complete the walk that Daniel cannot. He starts in Roncesvalles, Spain, near where Daniel died. Months later, he arrives in Santiago, Spain.

He is a changed man.

The terminus for the pilgrimage is the tomb of St. James, the cathedral church in Santiago. To complete their journey and get the final stamp in their pilgrimage passport, pilgrims must give a brief statement of why they undertook their journey.

In the movie, not one person at the end of their journey gives the same reason that they gave at the beginning of it. Joost, who started out wanting to lose weight, says he walked to reconcile with his wife. Sarah has quit smoking, her stated aim, but says she actually walked to find peace. Jack, who hated God when he began, says he has found his way back to God. And Tommy—Tommy now understands and loves his son.

It's not that any of them were lying earlier. It's just that they began the journey with only a partial understanding of why. Only by walking did they discover the reason they walked. Some of it was penance. Some of it was working through shame, anger, fear, unforgiveness. All of it was discovering a deep connection with others, with themselves, with God.

Whether it's a pilgrimage or a walk around the block, it's the reason you walk.

SETTING OUT

God Speed

PILGRIMAGE

In his book *The Road Is How: A Prairie Pilgrimage through Nature, Desire, and Soul*, Trevor Herriot documents a short pilgrimage he took on dusty roads past sodden fields on the outskirts of Regina, Saskatchewan. In some ways his journey was as unexotic as a meal at a gas station diner. His wife dropped him off about an hour from their doorstep, and for three days he walked on land flat as floors, in sun and rain, down old farm roads, across wide fields, through swampy bogs, past barking dogs. Sometimes his wife drove by, just to make sure he wasn't dead or suffering delusion from dehydration. At any point, he was never farther than a few miles from a store or a phone. He drank water that he'd left in jars along his route. It was surpassingly simple.

Yet those three days helped him to recover things he only vaguely knew he'd lost and to sort out things that troubled him deeply and to come back to himself, to re-member himself, and to find a way forward. It helped him, at least in part, answer a question he started with: "What do I do with my desire?"

Even pilgrimage—its own kind of vision quest—can be done on the cheap and likely without imperiling your life.

Going on pilgrimage yourself might take you a day or several, or a week or more. It will take, especially if it's more than a day, a bit of planning: what will you eat, where will you find

66

fresh water, where will you sleep, what will you do if you get blisters or rain comes at you slantwise or the sun starts making you hallucinatory? Will you pass through wild places? Do you need bear spray? Do you know what to do if you meet a moose in rut? How will you start a fire in wind or rain? Will you take your phone? If you do, will you use it aside from emergencies?

You likely want to head out with a question or two in hand, about your future or a present dilemma or, maybe, why you are the way you are and do the things you do. Be prepared that the question or questions might change along the way. And it's probably best not to press too hard for answers. It might be better to ask the questions as you set out but more or less forget them as you go along, or at least let them fall into that place in your brain where they do their work deeper than your analytical mind can box and quarantine them.

Because the road is how. Because it is cured by walking. Because it's the walking, the rhythm of it, its monotony, that stirs up the depths. It's dealing with weather and traffic and hunger and thirst and sore feet and dreams of a hot shower and a warm bed—it's all this, stretched out over a distance long enough to cause some discomfort, that makes you start to face yourself and maybe, on the way, find yourself.

MILE TWO

MAKING
TRACKS

*Thus you will walk in the ways of the good
and keep to the paths of the righteous.*

—PROVERBS 2:20

CHAPTER 6

Walking as Exercise

The most obvious thing about walking is that it's good for you. For your body. Your heart. Your mind. Take a walk and everything in you thanks you. Your blood gets oxygen. Your muscles too, plus they stretch and contract and knit back together more tightly. Your lungs do what lungs are created to do, breathe fresh air down to their roots, breathe out stale air for trees to do their magic with.

Walking is exercise.

An interesting word, *exercise*. We exercise an idea or an opinion or a reflection when we turn it into action, even if that action is merely speech. But mostly, the word conjures a picture of vigorous physical activity, activity that gets your heart thumping, your sweat glands opening, your insides burning. Working out. Training up. Pushing through. The word carries, way down in its Latin roots, the idea of both exertion and restraint. To exercise is to let loose but also to hold back. It is abandon and discipline all tied together. To exercise an idea is not to rant. To exercise a limb is not to flail. It is to push yourself within a fixed boundary: make this speech, run that path, curl these weights, shimmy this rope.

Someone exercising is at one and the same time pushing themselves and containing themselves. A man doing chin-ups or a woman cross-country skiing or a child swinging, arm over arm, on monkey bars—each is a study in abandon and discipline.

Most exercise is intentional. We set time aside for it. We usually go to a place to do it. I have an exercise routine I do six days a week, with some variation. If I'm at home, it's always in the same place, a corner of my home office. If I'm traveling, I find space somewhere, usually at the foot of my hotel bed. My exercise involves all the usual stuff: raising the heart rate, working the core, covering the muscle groups, lathering up a sweat. I skip, I squat, I bend, I crunch. I grunt. It's how I keep my girlish figure, in case you were wondering.

Walking is both this and something else. Obviously, many people walk for exercise. I remember a diet-and-exercise fad sweeping through my town, many years ago now, and the main, maybe only, form of exercise involved was walking. But not just any walking; this was borderline marching—a fixed determination, eyes set straight ahead, a brisk and purposeful charging forth, arms swinging with martial vigor. For sixty minutes every day. Over the next few months, a veritable army of walkers appeared at all hours on streets and paths, in parks, in malls, all blazing about the place like field marshals, bent toward some urgent task.

Then one by one, then ten by ten, then drove by drove, they disappeared. I think it got cold. Or the routine got dull or took too long or was too slow in producing results. Or they fell back in love with whatever kind of food they had, for a season, forsaken, and now why bother with any of it? I would picture some of them sitting in front of the television right at the time they used to walk, a bowl of something salty and fatty on their laps, feeling that little twinge of misery we experience when we've had something good and then lost it.

I know, because, though I never got swept up in that particular diet-and-exercise fad, I have made, more than once, vows to walk daily, with vigor and purpose and for significant distances. And I have kept it up. For a week, once for nearly two. Then one day it was raining. Or my ankle twisted stepping off a curb and I needed to stay off it. Or I really had only this evening to get my taxes done, and I couldn't do both, walking and taxes. The government forces me to do only one of these. What option did I have?

All's to say, walking has never been, beyond these sporadic bursts of commitment, my go-to exercise.

But still, I walk every day. Sometimes it's not much: up and down the stairs several times (mind you, we have nine-foot ceilings, so that extra couple of stairs really helps), between rooms, across floors. I walk to and from my car and across the big lot where I work, and at least once a week over to the coffee place on the next corner. On any given day, without intending to, I walk at least a mile, maybe two. Other times, it's more: I walk with a friend around a lake or to my appointment instead of driving, or go out on the hoof to clear my head, get some air, shake off the midday drowsies.

None of it is done to get or stay in shape. Little of it is done on purpose. But all of it is exercise. The exercise is a side effect of some other intent.

THE BENEFITS OF WALKING

But what actually happens when we walk? The list of benefits is long and impressive. Walking is medicine, therapy, and workout all bundled together. Compared to her sedentary neighbor, a walker lives longer in a better mood with a stronger heart and less girth on the bone. She has a keener mind, a clearer memory, a happier outlook. She's less likely to suffer stroke, heart attack, or angina. She has lower cholesterol and blood pressure. She has reduced risk of diabetes, cancer, depression, anxiety, and dementia. She is less drowsy in the day, sleeps better in the night, and has more energy for everything.

Walking is a miracle of physiology—a single step involves a dazzling artistry of neurons, muscles, heart, lungs, equilibrium, and bone density all working together. But walking also is a boon to health—a twenty- to thirty-minute walk a day, at a moderate pace, gives all these benefits and more.

Dr. JoAnn E. Manson of the Harvard Medical School says, "If there was a pill that people could take that would nearly cut in half the risk of stroke, diabetes, heart disease, reduce the risk of cognitive decline, depression, reduce stress, improve emotional well-being—everyone would be clamoring to take it, it would be flying off the shelf. But that pill, that magic potion, really is available to everyone in the form of thirty minutes a day of brisk walking."[17]

Dr. Manson says that walking is one of the main prescriptions she dispenses for people with various emotional, mental, and physical ailments.

All of which makes me wonder why I am not walking more for the sheer goodness of it.

So a fresh resolve, and this time I mean it. I am going to walk on purpose, and even if it's for other reasons—to visit a friend, work out a problem, pay more attention—I'm also going to do it for the sheer goodness of the thing.

THE TREES OF THE FIELD WILL CLAP THEIR HANDS

Most of us have a deep hunch, and a handful of supporting anecdotes, that walking in nature perks us up more than walking in a city—or certainly more than doing laps around a track or taking a thousand steps on a stationary device. We notice that strolling down a forest trail or trekking up a mountain path shakes off the doldrums quicker, and more lastingly, than dodging sidewalk pedestrians or trudging on a treadmill. We tend to go from sluggish to alert, from bored to engaged, from anxious to peaceful most times that we go God speed. It just comes sooner and goes deeper when big trees or arching skies or grassy fields are involved.

The hunch, it turns out, is correct. Nature is good for our overall health, body and mind. One researcher says that exercising in nature is "exercise squared."[18] Some of this, no doubt, is psychological: forests and mountains and rivers and oceans usually lift the soul more than buildings and crowds and traffic and asphalt do. And some of nature's benefits for the body are obvious: fresh air laden with the scent of pine or cedar or glacier or lavender, tumbling down great heights, sweeping across wild oceans, winding through steep valleys before arriving in your lungs—that is pure tonic, and much better for you than the often stale air of city streets, thick with all of its fumes and gases. More on that in a moment.

And walking or running on a variety of uneven surfaces—a carpet of fallen leaves, a trail raddled with tree roots, a moonscape of sandstone, sand pounded smooth and slightly pleated by waves—uses more of our muscles, calibrates better our equilibrium, increases our circulation, and is easier on our joints than running, say, on cement.[19]

But there's more. Trees and plants absorb poisons—carbon monoxide, carbon dioxide, plus the massive amounts of volatile or toxic particles emitted by many things all around us: paints, carpets, computers, hair spray. Plants are the lungs of nature. We have known this for a long time.

What we now also know is that plants emit, through their fragrances, particles called phytoncides. These are natural-born killers, but in a good way. They protect a plant from insects and diseases. But they also do that for us. When we breathe in the scent of a cedar tree or a lavender field, we also breathe in the plant's phytoncides. These increase our immunity, often significantly, multiplying white blood cells. Phytoncides protect us, just as they do the plant, from many nasty things floating around meaning us harm.[20] A new fad called forest bathing has come out of this. But it's got deep roots in Japanese culture, where it's called *shinrin-yoku.* Something like this has also been part of the traditional ways of Coast Salish people along North America's west coast.

But it works. The mounting studies on the health benefits of being in nature, especially when combined with exercise, are overwhelming.[21]

Not all of us can take our exercise in primeval forests or beside crashing seascapes or down sleepy country lanes. But usually even the most urbanized of us has a park only a block or three away. Can you walk there?

The prophet Isaiah, approaching the crescendo of his vision of God and God's word redeeming and renewing all creation, says,

> You will go out in joy
>> and be led forth in peace;
> the mountains and hills
>> will burst into song before you,
> and all the trees of the field
>> will clap their hands.

—ISAIAH 55:12

God has created creation to celebrate with us his redemption of us. Creation will clap with our clapping, sing with our singing, dance with our dancing, shout with our shouting.

Well, you may as well go get a head start. You may as well exercise that idea now.

God Speed

THE LUCK OF FINDING THE PARKING SPOT FARTHEST FROM THE MALL

All my life I've been in a rush.

I hurry even when I have nowhere to go. I hurry even without a deadline. I hurry not out of a desire to be punctual but out of some deeper need: because hurry is in my bones, thick, breeding, aching all the time. I hurry not because I need to but just because that's how I get from one place to the next.

I hurry because I have hurry sickness.

So I look for the parking spot closest to the mall or wherever it is I'm going (which, actually, is rarely the mall). A restaurant? The spot right at the curb, please. A fly-fishing shop? The place nearest the entrance, thanks. The bakery? Is there a drive-through? The airport long-stay lot? I have my eye on that short row of stalls right beside the terminal sidewalk.

But everyone, it seems, wants that spot too. It's a jousting match to get it. There we all are, jockeying for position, circling the same huddle of parked vehicles in the anxious hope that space will open up, *terra nullius*, between the green van and the black sedan, and *I will be the one to seize it*. There is a whole collection of videos on YouTube of people yelling, shoving, sometimes brawling in parking lots over territorial claims to parking spots.

We all want to be the lucky one who finds the spot closest to the mall.

Only recently have I discovered the luck of finding the parking spot farthest away. Most parking lots have an outer fringe, a far and lonely side, where few venture. There is no competition for space here. There is no circling and jockeying. There are no shouting matches and fistfights. There is just row on row of elegant emptiness, like a Kazimir Malevich painting or a winter prairie landscape. You can take your pick of places to park. If you're one of those annoying people who straddle two stalls, you can do that here with no one noticing or caring or being tempted to key three panels of your vehicle or pop your tires with a jackknife as some kind of cosmic payback.

I am training myself to seek this outer fringe. My anxiety here is nil. All that room, all those available spaces, all that horizon. My happiness is extravagant. It is the same happiness I feel when I win something, as opposed to what I feel when I nab the spot that the other driver is trying for, which is roughly the feeling of getting something by stealing or lying.

That back lot is an abandoned gold mine with untapped seams, there for the taking.

The best part is I get a long walk out of it. I get exercise. And I get all that comes with walking: fresh air, time to reflect, space to see more clearly.

The exercise part I've just written about. But the reflection part is worth some consideration. Let's say I am going to the mall. And let's say I'm going because I'm in the grip of coveting. I'm heading for a binge. I want—nay, need—some stuff to fill up the existential abyss in me. My wallet is burning a hole in my pocket. My hands itch to hold something new and shiny.

But there I am, way back in the parking lot, walking, thinking. Gaining perspective. Sorting out my needs from my wants. Feeling the earth beneath my feet, even if it's covered in ten acres of asphalt: even this gives me some grounding.

What usually happens is I leave as empty-handed as I came. I walk the long walk back to my car. Sometimes humming a song. Always, giving thanks. I'm thankful for many things—for legs that still work, for a car out there on the far edge of civilization, for a home to drive to, for a beautiful wife in that home, and for all the things I already have, so many things that I really don't need more.

I feel so lucky finding the parking spot farthest from the mall. But there's more than enough for both of us, for all of us. So my recommendation: on your next visit to the mall, go find that spot too.

CHAPTER 7

Walking as Friendship

I no longer call you servants, because a servant does not know his master's business," Jesus said to his disciples the night before his death. "Instead, I have called you friends, for everything that I learned from my Father I have made known to you" (John 15:15).

Jesus says this while sitting with his disciples around a table spread with the remnants of a meal: a gleaming shank of bone, a hunk of torn bread, a scattering of crumbs, the dark pits of olives, goblets stained by wine. They're inside, and upstairs, reclining. So it's easy to miss the obvious: that Jesus made known to them the things he learned from his Father not mostly in rooms around tables but afoot, under open sky, amid the clack of gravel, the barking of dogs, the laughter of children. The wind sometimes winged away his words and he had to repeat himself. Some nights the cold cut to the bone. Some days the heat pressed like an iron. Someone's muscle spasmed, another's knee locked, another's shin ached.

All got blisters.

Picture them. For long stretches they are silent, each thinking his own thoughts, doubt niggling their faith, fear testing their courage. They're hungry more times than not. Sometimes they banter, talk about that funny woman who sold them bread in the last village or those two old men kvetching about the price of olive oil. Sometimes they argue, bickering over who gets the straw bed tonight. When they're grumpy, they spread out along the road, keep their distance. Peter, more eager than fit, is almost always out of breath. John, testy and cocky, needs to be out front. Bartholomew dawdles, is easily distracted. Thomas is steady, neither fast nor slow. Judas takes up the rear, deliberately lags behind, watches everyone.

Then Jesus starts to speak. "The Father showed me something this morning." And there they all are, knotting around him, even Judas, jostling for position, straining to hear. They ask him to repeat words they miss or explain ideas that mystify them. They ask him to say more. Tell another story. When he stops speaking and they run out of questions, each one spreads out again, pondering it all. Two or three carry on a conversation, weighing what they've heard, making out its meaning, figuring out its implications. Others crawl up inside themselves, disturbed, puzzled, amazed.

They walk, they listen, they ponder, they discuss. They push back, sometimes pull away. They laugh and joke. They squabble and obsess. They cook up conspiracy theories. They stretch the truth. They grow wary, they get hurt, become lonely. They risk vulnerability and, afterward, sometimes regret it.

They discover all the way along the strange messiness of friendship. It comes by push and pull, in fits and starts. It's a rhythm of commitment and estrangement. Servants don't know their master's business. They just carry out orders. But friends, everything they learn they make known to each other. We mind each other's business, with all the surprise and subversion of that. Friends don't carry out orders. It's better than that, and worse: friends meddle in one another's lives. Friends aren't always friendly. Friends don't always even like one another. It's not uncommon for friends to resent each other.

What makes it friendship is we keep walking together.

So much of this minding each other's business—this meddling in each other's lives—happens on the way. Of course, much of it happens in rooms, around tables. We sit and talk over meals or drinks. We encounter each other in restaurants and kitchens and living rooms and classrooms. All this is good and well. But when we dare to risk taking a relationship deeper, usually we walk together.

Walking together feels more intimate and vulnerable than sitting across a table from each other, though that is intimate and vulnerable too. Maybe it's enough to say that walking alongside another person opens up space differently from sitting face to face with them. When we walk together we encounter the world together. The dynamics of that—you beside me, me beside you, the earth beneath us, the sky above us, the world around us, the road before us—alters how we speak and listen and see and think. There's more going on. We're not just verbal but kinetic. The scene keeps changing. All this is more evocative than just sitting talking. Most of us are more inclined to remember a conversation had while walking than one had otherwise.

And walking often invites greater candor and disclosure. I can't say exactly why this might be so, except that maybe every act of walking, no matter how short in distance and duration, is a kind of journey, and journeys have a way of loosening us up and prying us open. Journeys carry a hint of risk. We might get mugged or bit by a dog or run over, or lose our passport or our way, or contract malaria or freeze to death or suffer heatstroke. We might trip and break our collarbone. Also, walking takes effort. That combination—the risk, the effort—is its own kind of vulnerability. Maybe, sensing all this, we think, *Okay, why not venture some emotional vulnerability too?*

At any rate, when Jesus told his disciples they were no longer his servants but his friends, he said it while sitting down, but almost for sure the transformation from servants to friends happened afoot, one step at a time, mile on mile on mile.

They embarked as a master with his servants.

They arrived as friends.

Much walking lay between the two.

MIMICRY AND RIVALRY

Famed critic and cultural theorist René Girard created a theory of friendship that goes something like this: the more we like someone, the more we become like them and they like us. We mimic each other. We subtly or openly encourage this mimicry, inviting our friend to love what we love, to do what we do, to seek what we seek. But the more we mimic each other, the more we risk becoming rivals with one another. Estrangement lurks beneath every friendship. Closeness carries the seeds of competition.

Imagine you and I meet and we hit it off. You're, let's say, an avid birdwatcher, and I love motorcycles. After the friendship's underway, I invite you to a motorcycle show and enthuse over bikes, bike apparel, bike apparatus. I suggest, subtly or blatantly, that you buy a bike. How much fun we could have—how richer and deeper our friendship could be—if we took to the open road together.

Meanwhile, you're doing the same with birds. You take me to a binocular store and explain to me why this pair is superior to that one. You show me your various tattered guidebooks, and particularly the one you inherited from your grandfather on wading birds of the Pacific Northwest. That's your special passion. You show me a YouTube video of people up at dawn, wading marshes, their breath steaming on cold air, hoping to get a glimpse of some rare species of heron. You show me another video of techniques for squawking or warbling or cawing like this bird or that.

Let's say we convince each other. Every weekend, we ride our motorcycles together to visit bird sanctuaries. A rich friendship emerges. We bend into each other's lives. We mimic each other's passions. We meddle in each other's lives, mind each other's business.

But let's say you're better at motorcycles than I am, whatever exactly that means. You become more of a motorcycle aficionado than me. Plus you have a cooler bike and study to know every intimate detail of it, and on top of that are a more skillful rider than I am. Before too long, you've taken the lead. You're instructing me on all things motorcycle. Your motorcycle lore and skill and fervor surpass mine in every way. You start going to motorcycle shows without me. You find other people to ride with, people who can keep up.

I resent you for this.

And why shouldn't I? I'm the one who got you into

motorcycles to begin with. If not for me, you would have been just another trudging, boring half-asleep driver, coddled behind the wheel, strapped and trussed and girded, protected by air bags ready to inflate at the slightest hint of trouble. Yours was always only a pampered existence, out of the wind. It was me, the one born to be wild, who showed you the light. My shining virtue saved you from a life of wretched dullness. And now you preen about like Lord Harley himself.

The nerve of it.

We see all this—this mimicry leading to rivalry—in Jesus' disciples. Maybe not so much in their friendship with Jesus—though there are hints of that—but certainly in their friendship with one another. They are so different from one another when they first set out—a handful of fishermen, a zealot, maybe two, a tax collector, whatever Thomas is, and so on. We get brief but vivid glimpses of their varied personalities: Peter's impetuousness, John's hotheadedness, Thomas's severity, Andrew's little-brother syndrome. But more and more, they become alike. And as they do, the tensions between them brew, the frictions spark, the fights erupt. They mimic their way into rivalry. The question that finally explodes into open argument—"Who is greatest?"—can emerge only among those vying for the same turf. A violinist and a dentist have little in common but nothing to fight over. But two violinists? That's a showdown waiting to happen. Matthew and Simon, one a tax collector and the other a zealot, would have initially hated each other for being so different from one another, for loving such opposite things. But later, they might have hated each other for being so alike, for loving the same things. And that second hatred would have been the deeper of the two, the one with rustier, sharper barbs in it.

But it all came around. By the end, even Jesus' own brothers, who during his lifetime thought he was bonkers, had signed up. Even Peter and Paul, two men with big personalities and a need to be in the lead, seemed to have hammered out a working relationship. Matthew and Simon likely went on vacations together.

Because the one friendship that redeems—or at least can redeem—all friendships is the one we have with Jesus. The mimicry that Jesus invites us to—follow me, learn from me, take my yoke upon you—never distorts our personality; it releases it. We become more ourselves by becoming more like Jesus. Though it's possible to have moments of rivalry with Jesus, it's rare. Mostly we experience freedom. We lose our life but gain it. We speak his words, and find our voice. We walk in his ways, and hit our stride. We conform to his character, and discover our true selves. We submit to his will, and stop being slaves to everyone else's, our own especially.

And the more that happens, the more we mimic Jesus and so become our real selves, the less others threaten or annoy us. Because Jesus frees us to become ourselves, we are free to be different from others, and equally free to be similar to others. We can be friends without being rivals. Our friendship with Jesus gives us strength and humility to stop competing, stop one-upping, stop proving ourselves and strutting our stuff. We can love, you and I, the same things, and love that we love the same things.

Because of Jesus, I love that you love motorcycles. I hope you don't mind I never really got into birdwatching.

But most of us won't get here, to this depth of friendship free of rivalry, without some walking.

SURRENDERING ALL

There's an ancient friendship that still captures our imagination. It's Jonathan and David. The story of their friendship is scattered over several chapters in 1 Samuel (1 Sam. 18–20; 23:15–18). The bits and pieces give us a series of vivid glimpses into something remarkable. The friendship starts without warning, right after David kills Goliath and speaks with Jonathan's father, King Saul, about it. "After David had finished talking with Saul, Jonathan became one in spirit with David, and he loved him as himself. . . . And Jonathan made a covenant with David because he loved him as himself. Jonathan took off the robe he was wearing and gave it to David, along with his tunic, and even his sword, his bow and his belt" (1 Sam. 18:1–4).

We don't see this coming. Jonathan appears from nowhere and starts throwing away his future.

And even his sword. Jonathan disarms himself. He strips himself of all defenses in the presence of David. On his first meeting with David, he virtually abdicates his right to the throne: robe, tunic, sword, bow, belt.[22] All his insignia. All the trappings of his princedom. Later, Saul will also strip himself of his royal garments, strip himself naked, in the presence of David and the prophet Samuel. The implications of that are clear: Saul is undone, divested of his kingly power, devoid of all regal bearing. The thundering sovereign becomes a babbling child lying athwart the earth (1 Sam. 19:23–24). Saul suffers this fate unbidden, unwillingly. It is an act of divine humiliation. It is forced on him. But Jonathan embraces this condition voluntarily, joyously, spontaneously. It is an act of self-humiliation. He chooses it.

It's not as though Jonathan hobbled beneath an inferiority

complex. He didn't speak with a stammer, run from his own shadow. He is every inch a king. He has all it takes, and then some, to be Israel's next leader. Long before we ever meet David, we meet Jonathan, and he is awesome. He's everything his father, Saul, used to be but lost: brave, daring, humble, decisive. Jonathan leads men by winning their hearts, unlike Saul, who demands loyalty by threats and manipulation. Jonathan fights and routs Philistines when Saul dithers and whirls in fits of superstition. He defies his father's bizarre order to fast while the battle is joined. And when he is found out, Saul's own soldiers defy the king to defend Jonathan. (See 1 Sam. 13:23–14:46.) Jonathan, actually, is a man after God's own heart.

And he has the most to lose. Jonathan is, after all, heir to the throne. A king in waiting. David is never a threat to Saul's kingship; Saul reigns until his own death. But David is a threat to Saul's dynastic rule, the establishing of a kingly line. David threatens Jonathan's future, not Saul's present.

Yet the first time Jonathan meets David, he throws it all away. *And even his sword.* All, every symbol of his royal power, he surrenders to David. Like his namesake John the Baptist with Jesus, Jonathan becomes less so that David can become greater. He makes himself the groomsman to David's bridegroom. He makes himself the pageboy at David's coronation.

He could easily arrange for David's death and gain the throne. Instead, he lays the groundwork for David's ascension and abdicates his own throne.

The last time David and Jonathan meet is in a cave in the desert. Saul, in his mad cunning, tracks David to kill him. But Saul can't locate David despite marshaling all the resources of empire to attempt it. He has tracking dogs, drones, satellites, moles, crack operatives on the ground. He's got state-of-the-art surveillance equipment. All draw a blank.

But Jonathan, not even breaking a sweat, walks straight up to David's hidey-hole and greets him. Deep calls to deep.

Here's the scene: "While David was at Horesh in the Desert of Ziph, he learned that Saul had come out to take his life. And Saul's son Jonathan went to David at Horesh and helped him find strength in God. 'Don't be afraid,' he said. 'My father Saul will not lay a hand on you. You will be king over Israel, and I will be second to you. Even my father knows this'" (1 Sam. 23:15–17).

That's the last they ever see one another. Many years later, Jonathan dies in battle against the Philistines. David laments him. Later still, David fulfills a promised kindness to Jonathan by seeking and providing for Jonathan's one living son, Mephibosheth. But David, after Horesh, never sees or speaks with Jonathan again.

I wonder if he pondered Jonathan's parting words to him: *And I will be second to you.*

This is the role Jonathan chose. No one forced it on him. No threat was attached to his refusing it. It came at great expense. And at the time he chose it, it made little sense. After their final encounter, David didn't become king of Judah for at least a decade, maybe twelve years. And then it took another seven years after that to be made king of Israel, Saul's territory, and Jonathan's. David did not sit on Saul's throne for nearly two decades after Jonathan predicted he would.

And yet Jonathan surrendered all for it when they had barely met.

This friendship is the opposite of what Girard describes. The sameness between Jonathan and David—both gifted, both beloved, both skillful warriors, both kingly—does not create rivalry but relinquishment, at least for Jonathan. For Jonathan, mimicry awakens not competition but surrender. David is great in all the same ways Jonathan is great, but it does not arouse jealousy in Jonathan like it does in his father, Saul. Instead, it calls forth deepest servanthood. Though in very nature a king, Jonathan does not consider equality with the king something to be grasped but instead humbles himself and becomes in very nature a servant.

And note well that David and Jonathan's friendship is unlike most of ours in this one particular: any rivalry between us usually has nothing much at stake, except maybe a little ego. It doesn't really matter if you ride a motorcycle better than I do or I get better birdwatching binoculars than you have.

But Jonathan? For friendship he relinquished a kingdom.

AN EVEN DEEPER FRIENDSHIP

Surely this anticipates Christ in many layered ways. Though Jesus is the "son of David," it's Jonathan who most models Jesus' self-giving love.

But let me draw something else out.

Jonathan seems immune to jealousy and rivalry in his friendship with David. Why? That immunity must have a root, something it's anchored to, something it draws life from. We get only fleeting glimpses of Jonathan's relationship with his father, Saul, but the glimpses we do get—Saul calls him the "son of a rebellious woman" and twice he tries to kill him—don't give the impression that theirs was a deeply close and nourishing relationship.

One clue we have is from the portion of Scripture I just cited: "And Jonathan helped [David] find strength in God." Jonathan could not have helped David in this way if he didn't know how to find such strength himself. In his times of fear, of anxiety, of uncertainty, of sorrow, of loneliness, he must have found a well. He must have had a path. He must have known all the shortcuts to God's presence.

This is basing a lot on a little, but my guess is that Jonathan's extraordinary capacity to relinquish treasured things, valuable things, inherited things for the sake of his friend David came out of yet a deeper friendship. It came from walking with God.

That's a wild guess, I know.

Or maybe not.

Maybe that's how any of us gets free from our pettiness. Free from our thin skins. Free from our need to be admired by others. Free from our craving to be better than others. Maybe the only way any of us gives up a piece of ourselves, *even our swords*, is by a long way walking with the one who gave himself up, *even his own life*, just to make us his treasure and to make us like he is. To make us a royal priesthood.

Maybe no one truly becomes themselves—wholly, freely, unreservedly, not needing to be someone else—until we walk long enough with Jesus that we become as he is.

God Speed

"I WILL GO WITH YOU, MR. FRODO"

When I was ten, my father returned from a business trip with a new find. He worked back then for a big oil company. He pounded thousands of miles on barren northern highways and winding gravel roads, all along the way talking to truckers and loggers and excavators about fuels and lubricants. That man knew more about oil—how it was extracted and refined, its thickness or thinness at various temperatures, what this or that additive did to it—than anyone I've ever met. Also, my dad had a golden tongue and a massive vocabulary, so he could make it all sound epic and poetic. He would say the word *viscosity* with such poignancy it would make you want to weep. He was the Shakespeare of petroleum products.

Which is all to say, my dad had finely tuned literary sensibilities even though his formal education was limited and his day job didn't encourage artistic ambitions. But he loved great literature, and when I was ten he gave me a book he said was a masterpiece. I believed him and started reading it straightaway, and fell under its spell completely.

The book's name: *The Lord of the Rings* by J. R. R. Tolkien.

Since then, I've read the trilogy several more times, and each time it keeps doing its work in me. Often, when I am up against some challenge or another, I often think of the various scenes and characters from *LoTR* and take my cues from that. How does Aragorn rally those with fragile hope?

How does Gandalf face insurmountable obstacles? How does Gimli overcome his centuries-old inbred prejudices?

And this: how does friendship work?

Tolkien knows something about this, or at least has an inkling. In *LoTR*, he depicts several rich and layered friendships, especially the one between the dwarf Gimli and the elf Legolas, which is a study in overcoming deep personal suspicions, historic animosity, and ethnic pride and forging enduring companionship.

But the friendship at the center of the story is between two hobbits, Frodo Baggins and his gardener, Sam Gamgee, or Samwise. It is between a servant and his master. It is sometimes as hard, or harder, to overcome social barriers as it is other ones—racial, generational, cultural, economic. How many wealthy women become friends with their maids? How many high-level financiers go boating with their mechanics? It's rare.

Sam and Frodo become unlikely friends. We can't imagine it happening had a crisis not crashed into their world. That crisis called them to tasks they otherwise never would have imagined or sought. But as Gandalf says to Frodo, "All we have to decide is what to do with the time that is given us."

Their friendship, Sam and Frodo's, emerges slowly, and awkwardly.

And it comes by walking. It takes a long time and many miles for both of them to break free of the socially constructed roles they inhabit. The moment when their relationship starts to become a friendship—when Frodo begins to see Sam as an equal and not just an underling—is when Frodo decides to make the journey to Mordor and chooses to go it alone. But Sam insists on coming with him, even though he knows that they will likely never return.

The friendship really starts when they walk into the deepening darkness with little hope that they will ever make it back to the light.

"I will go with you, Mr. Frodo," is how Sam announces this—simple, humble, folksy. And dead earnest. It is not a question. The servant dares to instruct the master. Frodo seems both relieved and annoyed. But the friendship proves essential to completing the almost impossible mission: getting into the evil kingdom of Mordor and destroying the ring of power—which has Frodo in its thrall—at its fiery source. Without Sam, without his loyalty and endurance, Frodo likely would have perished on the way and certainly never would have finished what he started. He instead would have been consumed by the evil he set out to destroy.

"I will go with you, Mr. Frodo."

So much is underneath this. This is not any journey. This is walking toward death. This is choosing to be alongside someone on a journey from which there may be no coming back, literally and figuratively. Later, when the weight of the task gets too heavy for Frodo, Sam says, "I can't carry the ring, Mr. Frodo, but I can carry you." And he does.

I am not good at this depth of friendship.

My wife, though, is. In another of my books, I told some of the story of Cheryl's friendship with Carol, my pastoral colleague.[23] Carol made a long journey into darkness. She was diagnosed, days after her fortieth birthday, with a brain tumor, and for almost two years after that she walked toward death. Cheryl went every step of the way with her: the bad news, the bursts of short-lived good news, the pain, the drugs, the treatments, the physical, emotional, and personality changes that all those things brought. Cheryl didn't miss a step.

"I will go with you," Cheryl kept saying, even as the landscape became bleaker, the sky grimmer, the weight of it more oppressive. It was a journey Carol did not come back from, not on this side, and that Cheryl returned from only slowly, and altered.

It's worth noticing that when Jesus says to his disciples, "I no longer call you servants but friends," he's having his last meal with them before his death. He knows what's ahead and has tried his best to prepare his friends for it: he's going to destroy evil at its source. He doesn't want servants at a time like this. He needs friends. Or even one. Just someone to walk with him. Someone who, though he can't carry the cross, can carry him who carries it.

His friends barely comprehend, which is to say not at all. Later, as Jesus sweats blood in the garden of Gethsemane and pleads with just one of his friends to keep company with him, they keep falling asleep. This, I fear, would be me.

But not Cheryl. She would have stayed up all night. She would have sweated some blood of her own. She would have walked all the way and not turned back.

"I will go with you. I will carry you."

Oh, to have such a friend.

On your next walk, who will you carry, wakeful, in thought, in prayer?

CHAPTER 8

Walking with Animals

Here is a strange sight I see in my neighborhood every day: a woman walking her cat. Each evening, just before or after the dinner hour, she does her rounds. Her cat, harnessed around its forepaws, saunters on its leash. It feigns aloofness, scowls with disdain. It walks, as cats are wont to do, with no fixed plan, and no sense of the giddy adventure or scent-driven mission dogs have. This cat is both indignant and bored.

The whole thing is just weird, and somehow wrong. But it's also kind of cool.

But here is another strange sight I see in large cities: one person walking an entire herd of dogs. When I first saw it, in Central Park, Manhattan, I recoiled. What kind of insanity possessed this man to own eight dogs, all different breeds—a squat bulldog, a spindly poodle, a muscular rottweiler, a thing that looked like an extra in *Star Wars*, and so on? I knew of Crazy Cat Ladies—both my daughters have aspirations in that direction, and my mother once showed strong symptoms of this condition—but I'd never heard of Crazy Dog Men. Dog lovers, yes: that's healthy, natural, godly, holy.

But eight dogs?

Then I saw a woman with five dogs, and another man with seven, and two more people each with nine. And it finally clicked: these were hired leashes. Apparently, in New York City, and many other places besides, there is a thriving business in dog-walking services. Walking a dog is one of the great burdens and great joys of having a dog. Dogs tend to be needy, hungry, lazy, messy, but everything in them wakes up when you say the word *walk*. All the dogs in my life could go from coma to ecstasy in a breath at just the least suggestion of the tiniest hint of the slightest possibility of a walk. And somehow that joy is infectious. Who could not be happy walking a dog?

Take, for example, Jack. Jack was a rescue dog we brought home when he was, by our best estimates, two-and-a-half years old. He had been through some kind of personal Bosnia: he was skittish, anxious, cowering when we needed him to be brave, aggressive when we needed him to be gentle. A man with a hat or anything resembling a stick sent him into a panic. He was a yellow lab, maybe with something else blended in, but he had nothing of a lab's friendly-silly eagerness. He was more like one of those angry edgy wiry-little rodent-sized dogs. "Jack," I'd say, without a hint of scolding in my voice. Rather than doing what every good and true lab does—bounding up, tongue lolling, tail wagging, quivering with excitement: yayaya!—Jack would lift his head warily, turn it slowly toward me, and look at me with a mix of dread and annoyance.

"What now?" he seemed to say.

But the least clink of a leash clasp sent him into paroxysms of joy. He could be dead asleep upstairs and hear the quietest chime of metal downstairs, and he'd leap up, claws scrambling on the floors above, and thunder down the staircase. He'd press into me, whirl around me. He'd be beside himself with joy. The first five minutes of our walk—this never diminished in all the time we had him—he was so excited to be afoot that he'd strain at the leash to the point of choking himself. "Heel, Jack, heel," I'd say repeatedly, like a tent revivalist, and entirely without effect. After five minutes, he'd calm, and—though never exactly heeling; that level of disciplined order seemed beyond both of us—he ambled at a companionable pace, and the rest was pure delight.

I couldn't imagine farming out this part of dog owning out. I realize that dog owners in Manhattan, and other large cities, probably work impossible hours that forbid this simple pleasure, so I'm not judging them, but even I, unfit a dog owner as I am, realize that walking a dog stands at the sacred core of having a dog.

A FAITHFUL FRIEND

The week I was writing this chapter, my friend Graham sent me a message with the sad news that Judge, his faithful canine friend for the past fourteen years, had died. I knew Judge since he was eight weeks old, a tumbling, sniffing little furball of cuteness. As he matured, he became a constant companion—a kind of mascot and guide—for Graham. When Graham and I went out scuba diving or prawning on his boat, there was Judge: at boat's stern, like a second mate sillier than Gilligan, his whole body shaking with giddy anticipation. Even in his dotage, when his old body was weighed with years and slowed by arthritis, Judge was always an eager if somewhat hobbling host.

The deep sadness of losing Judge began for Graham several months before Judge died. That was when Judge became too old and stiff to do their daily walks. These walks were as much for Graham, maybe more so, as they were for Judge, though Judge loved them with as pure a love as any earthbound creature can love a thing. Graham rose each day, even weekends, at first light, and before anything—coffee, food, shower—he and Judge were out the door. Graham lives beside a large forest (well, he lives in British Columbia, where virtually everyone lives beside a large forest) that flanks a goodly sized mountain, and their route every day was the same: up the trail to the lake at the top, and then down the trail on the other side. Maybe two miles altogether. It was a tough climb—well, tough for Graham; in Judge's first years, he'd run up, run back, run up again, over and over. He'd snoop in the woods, chase a deer, flush some quail, sniff the remains of some owl's quarry, come lopping back grinning, his muzzle all besmirched. The journey home was easy as a slide, and both of them strode it with easy confidence. Graham used the whole time to pray, to muse, to work out personal and professional things, things that hurt him or angered him or bewildered him, dreams he had. Those walks got his mind clear, his heart pure, his faith solid.

They'd get back to the house still early in the morning, bursting through the door like Odysseus returning from his long tumultuous voyage. Anneke, Graham's wife, would have the coffee on. He'd shower, eat something, nurse a cup of coffee, read. Judge would flop down and curl up at the foot of his chair, and start snoring.

In those fourteen years, Graham went through stuff. He lost a business. He took up a public role that put him in the crosshairs of angry people. He had a back injury that gave him—prone, sitting, walking, it didn't matter—chronic pain.

What kept him strong and focused and hopeful and resolute were those morning walks, and morning prayers, with Judge at his side, or at least somewhere in earshot. Even when Graham's back vexed him, the walks renewed him.

As Judge aged, he slowed. He didn't chase things. He didn't sniff things. He didn't run up and back. He ambled. Then shambled. Then trudged. Then hobbled. Then one sad hard day arrived when Graham woke and beckoned Judge for their daily ritual. Judge, lying on his side, lifted his head, gave him a dole-eyed and guilty look, and then simply laid his head back down and closed his eyes. He didn't have another step up that mountain left in him.

Graham continued to walk. But it was never the same.

Those walks, almost fourteen years of them, were a kind of daily healing, probably for both of them, but certainly for Graham. Some days, the walks were solely about the exercise, the companionship, the fresh air. But many days, they were about taking hold or letting go or getting through or figuring out. They were about finding courage or forgiveness or wisdom or humility.

And Judge was as good a companion as he could have asked for. As I said, walking a dog is at the sacred core of having a dog.

FAITHING YOUR PRACTICES

I teach a course annually in personal formation at the university where I work. Last time I taught it, I began this way:

You've likely come to the course expecting that it will be

about practicing your faith: learning disciplines, old and new, that strengthen your relationship with God. Praying, fasting, serving, reading Scripture, and so forth. And yes, it is that. We will look at ways men and women throughout the ages have practiced their faith, and we'll try many of these things out.

But this course is also about faithing your practices: discovering how the things you already do, most of them every day—sleeping, eating, taking a shower, driving, working, washing clothes, scrubbing dishes, paying bills—all present you with opportunities to deepen your relationship with God. We will look at how, right now, you are doing things that you probably seldom associate with the pursuit of God. But you can faith these practices.

Then we went around the room, and I asked each student to describe something they had done that very week where they experienced God in some way. One man colored with his three-year-old daughter, and all through he felt he had both wings and roots. Another man drove to work but instead of stewing over the traffic, he prayed for every driver he pulled up next to, asking God to bless that person, their work, their home, their life. A woman talked about cleaning her basement, a job she'd put off all summer and finally threw herself into, and she found a quiet joy in it.

Most of the students, though, met God while walking their dogs. That was, indeed, the dominant motif of our conversation: walking Brutus each morning along the pathway by the marsh behind her house, Linda sensed God speaking to her about taking a step of faith; walking little Gilda each evening over the trails in his local park, Ralph finally mustered the courage to forgive his father; walking Beamer sporadically, when she could squeeze in the time around her shift work, Solange found this was the one hour in each day when she could fully worship. On and on these stories went, each one a testament to the intimate surprises of God.

It got me curious, and I did a search to see how many times the word *dog* or *dogs* shows up in the Bible, and to see if they have a common theme. I was hoping that *dog* was a kind of code word for *God*.

I found that the Bible mentions dog or dogs more than forty times, but my hopes for a connection with God were utterly dashed. Not a single mention is good. *Dog* is a byword for cowards, cads, lowlifes, evildoers. When describing the animal itself, the Bible depicts dogs as violent strays and scavengers, often flea-bitten.[24] Either way, metaphor or depiction, the creatures' worst traits are underlined: A dog has ravenous hunger. It travels in scavenging packs. You throw it worthless or tainted meat, and it still eats it. It snarls, bares its teeth, begs, scrounges, licks up blood, barks when it shouldn't, fails to bark when it should. "Dead dog" is the meanest, lowest insult you can throw at someone.

It's not the least encouraging.[25]

There is one gospel story, however, where the figurative mention of dogs is at first negative and then, with a strange twist, positive. It's the story where Jesus meets a desperate mother who is not part of Israel. Here it is in full:

Jesus left that place and went to the vicinity of Tyre. He entered a house and did not want anyone to know it; yet he could not keep his presence secret. In fact, as soon as she heard about him, a woman whose little daughter was possessed by an impure spirit came and fell at his feet. The woman was a Greek, born in Syrian Phoenicia. She begged Jesus to drive the demon out of her daughter.

"First let the children eat all they want," he told her, "for it is not right to take the children's bread and toss it to the dogs."

"Lord," she replied, "even the dogs under the table eat the children's crumbs."

Then he told her, "For such a reply, you may go; the demon has left your daughter."

She went home and found her child lying on the bed, and the demon gone.

—MARK 7:24–30

Call me a dog, this plucky woman says. *Fine. I won't argue. But let me tell you, Mr. Jesus, what dogs are like: they waste nothing. Give me your crumbs, I'll treat them like steak.*

For this reply, Jesus says, *you may go. For this reply, you get the whole banquet.*

This woman pulls out one trait of a dog that other Scriptures decry but that she—and then Jesus—applauds: a dog is always hungry. A dog happily, even greedily, eats what others throw away. A dog never feels entitled. A dog is only ever grateful. A dog will take what it gets.

Is there a connection between a dog's bottomless hunger and finding God in the margins, in the in-between places? Only a few of my students in class that first day attested to meeting God in conventional ways—at church, in Bible studies, doing religious things. I'm sure that they do meet God in these places, doing these things. But what they spoke about was finding God elsewhere. In the crumbs. In the cracks. On the floor.

Walking the dog.

And maybe, without any of them really thinking about it, the dog helped them find God in places they least expected.

NAMING THE ANIMALS

Why do we seem to need animals? Maybe all this goes back to the beginning. God's first assignment to Adam as his agent and image bearer was to name all the animals. When God gives Adam this task, he seems to have more than taxonomy in mind: "The LORD God said, 'It is not good for the man to be alone. I will make a helper suitable for him.' Now the LORD God had formed out of the ground all the wild animals and all the birds in the sky. He brought them to the man to see what he would name them; and whatever the man called each living creature, that was its name. So the man gave names to all the livestock, the birds in the sky and all the wild animals. But for Adam no suitable helper was found" (Gen. 2:18–20).

Adam is not just naming animals. He's on a search. He needs, and longs for, a "suitable helper." It is a need and longing that is finally and only fulfilled when God creates Eve. But Genesis hints that both Adam and God are open to the possibility that a nonhuman might meet the need, fulfill the longing. God sees Adam's aloneness and straightaway gets the man busy naming animals. It seems an interruption, a distraction, from the urgent matter at hand: Adam needs a friend. A companion. A helper.

But is it an interruption? God has already made a lot of creatures. Platypuses. Wombats. Pachyderms. Wolves. Saber-toothed tigers. Those big-eared saucer-eyed things that live in the trees of the Amazon. And, of course, dogs. I imagine a yellow lab coming to Adam, fawning and wagging his tail.

As Adam sees each animal, ponders each, names each, he likely also considers a question about each: *Could you be my friend? Could I be fulfilled hanging out with you? If we walked together and talked together, would you heal the deep ache in me?*

But not one can. Adam finds no suitable helper throughout the entire animal kingdom. Not even the yellow lab.

But here's the thing: God seems to think it's worth a shot. He seems to set up the whole naming exercise to test the possibility that maybe, just maybe, one of his four-legged creations will be the answer to all that ails man. That it doesn't work out this way is almost beside the point. The point is, God thinks it's worth a try.

Maybe God knows something. Maybe he knows, because maybe he made it this way, that animals—some animals, at least; maybe not bats or pigs or anteaters or lizards—but some animals possess a capacity to heal our deep-down stuff, our aches and longings, our bentness and hollowness, our lostness and loneliness. This claim has ample evidence to back it up, not the least the effectiveness of dogs and horses and cats, and sometimes bunnies and ferrets, to help heal people from anxiety, trauma, tragedy, estrangement. The young woman abused by her father doesn't trust anyone, but a horse senses her broken heart and has unending patience and wisdom and begins the healing. A young man mixed up with drugs and gangs may not have anyone who trusts him, but a dog meets him and loves him where he is, for who he is, and shows an uncanny skill for leading him back to the light.

SOLACE AND COMPANIONSHIP

Maybe, when God created animals and had Adam name them, he knew that humans would need those creatures after the fall. When they lost touch with the creator, they could look upon his creation to see his might (the lion), his sense of humor (the ostrich), his creative genius and abundant goodwill and flights of fancy (all the birds of the heavens and the fishes of the sea). And when sin separates man and woman, God knew that many of them could find real solace from and companionship with an animal.

Consider my parents. My father and mother—Bruce and Joyce, to whom I've dedicated this book—were married thirty-eight years, sometimes companionably, other times less so. They lived together in seven different homes in five different communities. They had three children, each who married and who produced for them eight grandchildren. They suffered together, worked alongside each other, overcame some huge challenges, and made a way.

They laughed a lot and gave each other deep strength. I remember listening from my bed as they talked late into the night, dreaming together of all the things they would do. I'd fall asleep happy, filled with their fullness.

They also argued a lot and sometimes hurt each other with biting words and other times shut each other out with long stretches of cold silence. I remember listening from my bed as they bickered late into the night, blaming each other, and then—worst of all—clamming up. I'd fall asleep afraid, empty with their emptiness.

They were like each other and not like each other. Same and different.

In those times when they were distant, when the hurts they'd inflicted on each other made a wall between them, each sought solace in one of their pets—my dad a dog, my mom a cat. They would often talk to the animal more than to each other, confiding, discussing, musing aloud. Buttons would cock its tiny head, look puzzled at my dad as he soliloquized about some matter, bark a little bark to urge him on. Or Teddy would curl up on my mother's lap, purring, sleeping and rousing, sometimes plucking her pants with its claws—making dough, my mother called it—attentive in a distracted catlike way to her monologues.

In time, Mom and Dad recovered a rich companionability. They loved each other always—that was a given—and by the end got so that they liked each other too. They became best friends. But now the pets were included. Now the animals were part of their companionship. Now they had each other, and also Buttons and Teddy.

All of this makes me wonder about Adam and Eve. They argued—at least once, a harsh and accusatory set-to, full of blame and bitter words, with terrible consequences. I'm sure it's not the only time they fought (Genesis 3). Somehow, though, they worked it out and lived to love another day.

But it makes me wonder how they handled the in-between times. The days of fuming at each other, the long stretches of cold silence, Adam in his corner of the garden, Eve in hers, each feeling alone, each thinking the other should say sorry first, each wondering if they wouldn't be better off going their own way.

Did they talk to the animals then? Did Eve turn to a lioness and pour out her anger and grief? Did Adam sit down with a coyote and tell it all his frustrations? Did they muse aloud with one of the living creatures formed out of the dust of the ground, share dreams that they didn't want to discuss with one other?

Who knows?

What I do know, because I've seen it up close many times, and not just in my own family, is the solace we often find in the companionship of an animal, especially when human companionship fails, when people betray us, reject us, ignore us, avoid us.

Then, even then, God keeps bringing the animals to us, to see what we will name them. To see if any suitable helper can be found among them. They are not bone of our bone, flesh of our flesh. But they are part of God's good creation. Part of God's abounding grace.

And sometimes, when we walk with the animals, the loneliness goes away.

If you have an animal who gives you solace and companionship, maybe who walks with you, this is as good a time as any to say so, and to say thanks.

God Speed

SHEEP WALKING

Dogs aren't the only animals that can affect us. Maybe sheep can change us too.

David, of giant-slaying fame, took much solace from walking with sheep. The relationship between a shepherd and his sheep provided David with his richest and most evocative imagery about God. "The Lord is my shepherd," David begins his most famous psalm. "He makes me lie down in green pasture, he leads me beside quiet waters" (Ps. 23:1–2). What David does for a flock, God does for him. In another psalm, Asaph portrays David as God's shepherd, beginning to end:

> He chose David his servant
>> and took him from the sheep pens;
> from tending the sheep he brought him
>> to be the shepherd of his people Jacob,
>> of Israel his inheritance.
> And David shepherded them with integrity of heart;
>> with skillful hands he led them.
>
> **—PSALM 78:70–72**

David likely never felt welcomed or loved in his own household. His brothers resented him. His father marginalized him. His mother, if her almost complete absence in the biblical record is any indication, was no more than a shadow in his life.[26] David saw God as both his midwife and his nursemaid, and maybe as his mother:

> Yet you brought me out of the womb;
>> you made me trust in you, even at my
>> mother's breast.
> From birth I was cast on you;
>> from my mother's womb you have
>> been my God.
>
> **—PSALM 22:9–10**

Yet David's name means "beloved." And as a boy, and then as a man, he does not lack for confidence or show any sense that people's extraordinary devotion to him is misplaced. Where does such confidence come from? The obvious answer is that he didn't look to his father or mother or brothers or other humans to find his strength or worth or identity or approval. He looked to God. *From birth I was cast on you.*

God was the source of his strength and worth and identity and approval. But by what means did David find these things?

The evidence suggests it came from walking with sheep. David learned to look to God and to trust his voice, the same way his sheep learned to look to him and trust his.

The Lord is my shepherd, I shall not want.

It's possible that David learned most, maybe all, of his early lessons in seeking and trusting God not from a parent or a priest or a friend. He learned it, it seems, from sheep.

On your walk today, either with or without a canine (or feline?) companion, reflect on an experience you've had with one of God's creatures. What did this animal teach you about who God is—or about who you are in relationship to God?

CHAPTER 9

Walking as Prayer

O h, if I could only pray," Martin Luther said at one of his table talks, "the way this dog watches the meat. All his thoughts are concentrated on this piece of meat. Otherwise he has no thought, wish, or hope."[27]

Typical Luther: vivid, earthy, vulgar. And hard to forget.

It reminds me of my wife. The longing part, not the other stuff. She looks to prayer with no other thought, wish, or hope. All her thoughts are concentrated on it. She craves it. She falls on it with gusto and savors every bite. She gets to it as quick as she can and stays at it as long as she might. She devours everything in sight, and then looks around for more.

She is one hungry pray-er.

Me, not so much. I dither and stall and fiddle once I get down to it. I'm more a finicky cat with dry food, barely tolerating the stuff, merely sniffing at it and, with a kind of regal disdain, nibbling a piece or two now and then, but just as often turning my nose up.

Oh, if only I could pray the way my wife does.

I've discovered that sitting still doesn't help much. Cheryl has a place she usually prays, a high-backed chair in her study, and she can sit there for ages lost in wonder. I try this and fall asleep. But her prayer is a continual awakening. Sometimes she prays with other people over the phone or the internet. The prayers rise in fervor, in pitch, in urgency the longer they go on. It sounds like a descent of wings, an invasion of angels, a storming of barricades. And there I am, in my little corner, mumbling away, worrying as much as praying, trying to stay awake.

But walking, that's different. Then all my senses wake up and God draws near and heaven comes close. Then I storm the heavens. When I walk, I pray. The two things for me are almost one. As I'll explore in the next chapter, walking is attentiveness. It's noticing things little and big, close and far, inside and out, above and below. It tends to the earthly and the heavenly all at a go. Well, praying is all this too. I rarely need intentionally to pray when I walk; prayer arises naturally. It becomes my breath and heartbeat and footfall.

I take to it like a dog does to meat.

Later in this chapter, I'll talk about the practice of prayer walking, which I do as well, and with generally more success than prayer sitting. But first let me talk about walking *as* prayer, where prayer is the natural companion to walking, its irrepressible overflow.

PRAYER ON THE MOVE

The prayer life I've most tried to imitate is Tevya's, the patriarch in *Fiddler on the Roof*. He talks with God everywhere, face to face, friend to friend. His prayers are intimate, jovial, querulous, wondering. He thanks and gripes and puzzles. He confesses and he pleads. He complains and he concedes.

But he's always moving. None of his praying is done sitting. It's almost as if movement triggers his praying, that his legs are connected, by strings and latches and pulleys, to his heart and mouth: once his legs engage, the other parts join in.

That's how it is for me. When I walk, I pray. Prayer starts stirring the inmost places the minute I set out. I notice things—trees and wind and clouds and people, animals, winged things, groundlings, traffic, sounds, silence. This noticing, this attentiveness, is its own kind of a prayer. It is holding, open-palmed, all these things before God. Or, even more, it is seeing, open-eyed, all these things *with* God. One step, two, and soon longing and gratitude and wonder and petition are working their way up through me, almost bodily, mingling with my thoughts, fusing with my emotions, pressing toward speech. Before long, all of it, the walking, the noticing, the feeling, the thinking, the speaking, is praying. "I don't know exactly what a prayer is," writes poet Mary Oliver. "I do know how to pay attention."[28]

I walked this way yesterday—out the back door, then a brief little jaunt to the mailbox at the end of the alleyway, and then back along the loop of our street to my front door. A quarter mile at most. Took all of ten minutes. Hardly counts as exercise or even getting fresh air. But in that brief walk, I grew aware. I thought of my neighbors, each and all of them, and even saw and greeted a few. I saw some of their pets, a shaggy lazy dog, a bristly wary cat, another dog, wiry and yappy. I saw their houses and their cars and their garden plots. I wondered about them. Each of them has a story: wanting things, fearing things, chasing things, running from things. Each feels, probably in the span of a single day, joy and sadness and shame and hope and love and pain and a dozen other things. Some believe in God and some don't, or do but don't think about God much or clearly (if anyone does that). Some are seeking God right now to say *Thank you* or *Help* or *What?*

And soon, seeing all this, wondering all this, I was praying for all this—not out loud, not stopping to extend my hands in hieratic blessing, not even formulating the prayers into words, in my head or on my lips. At most I mumbled, "Oh, God." But I was lifting it all, bathing it all, inviting God's presence into it all.

I was praying.

I was, apart from the kneeling, doing what the apostle Paul does for the believers in Ephesus:

> For this reason I bow my knees before the Father, from whom every family in heaven and on earth is named, that according to the riches of his glory he may grant you to be strengthened with power through his Spirit in your inner being, so that Christ may dwell in your hearts through faith—that you, being rooted and grounded in love, may have strength to comprehend with all the saints what is the breadth and length and height and depth, and to know the love of Christ that surpasses knowledge, that you may be filled with all the fullness of God.

> —EPHESIANS 3:14–19 ESV

I might simply amend that to this: "And, *walking with* the Father, from whom all the families on earth derive their name, I ask . . ."

Is this odd? Is this peculiar to me? Well, you alone can

answer for yourself. But I venture a guess that for most of us, walking is so close to praying that, with minimal effort, we could marry the two and hardly notice where one ends and the other starts.

A PRAYER WALK

But it's good sometimes to tie together, on purpose, walking and praying—to set out on an actual prayer walk.

The church where I pastored did this a fair amount, mostly under the urging of my wife. Admittedly, we usually did these walks in summertime, in warm dry weather, and called it off when it rained, so our commitment to the kingdom of God coming on earth as it is in heaven was perhaps not absolute. We would gather, usually no more than a dozen of us, at a certain time in a certain place. We began with a general prayer, agreed to meet back at the same place in an hour, and then broke off into groups of two or three to walk through the community and pray for it.

Some of the praying we did out loud, though to passersby it probably sounded like we were merely chatting with one another. Much of our praying was silent. Sometimes we paused, but most times we moved, not fast, but not pokey, either. The point was to cover ample ground in good time. Once in a while, someone would get talking to a dog-walker or a woman watering her roses or a man shepherding his children and end up praying for them—for an illness in the home or a child gone wayward or a toxic work environment. It was surprising, when it did happen, how natural it was, for us and the person we prayed for. We hardly met anyone who was not wide open, after maybe a moment of awkwardness, to receive prayer for healing or blessing. Many people wept. Most hugged us afterward.

Friendships sometimes formed among those who walked and prayed together. It is, after all, an act of vulnerability and intimacy to pray with another person. Prayer comes from and speaks to deep places in us. Some prayers descend quickly from head to mouth and usually are spoken in a series of stock phrases: *Oh, God, I ask that you'd just protect and bless Joe as he drives to Williams Lake; keep him safe, O Lord.* But other prayers rise slow as a male bear emerging from his winter's sleep or fierce as a mother bear defending her cubs. These prayers come from storehouses of wild longing. They are stolen, it seems, off the altar of God's throne room. Some seem like prayers from God's own heart, uttered by God's own lips. They have a powerful effect on both those who speak them and those who hear them. They knit us together, fiercely, tenderly.

I came back from these walks deeply refreshed. It was an experience, I think, similar to what Jesus had with the Samaritan woman at the well. When the disciples left him to go fetch food in a nearby village, Jesus was hungry, weary, thirsty. When they returned with food, urging him to eat, he was already full and rested and satisfied. He had not tasted a bite, taken a break, or gotten even the drink of water he asked the woman to provide.

"I have food you know nothing about," he tells his disciples. Which puzzles them, literalists that they are. Does he have a secret stash? A shadow supplier? Did he turn stones to bread?

"My food," he tells them, "is to do the will of my father and to finish his work" (from John 4:27–38).

Prayer walking helped me in the same way. What I felt, what I think we all felt, returning from them, especially when they involved these chance encounters with strangers or moments of deep calling to deep with one another, was this fullness, this refreshment, this satisfaction: this food we too often knew nothing about, but which, once tasted, replenishes completely.

Did God change anything for the neighbors by those prayers? Did the spiritual climate in the community shift? It's hard to say. We were poor at following up, which is a nice way of saying we didn't at all. So we had no way of knowing whether crime decreased or illnesses abated or sadness and anger lost their strangleholds in the communities we walked and prayed through. But we did sense God's presence, in us, with us, around us.

The prayers—and the walking—changed us. It made us more sensitive to human need, our own and others. It made us less judgmental, more humble, less likely to jump to conclusions. We became better listeners and keener observers. We worked through much of our own stuff—our fears and worries and jealousies.

And maybe, just maybe, a few prodigals came home and some spouses reconciled and someone finally admitted they had a drinking problem and another cried out to God to reveal himself and he did. Would such things have happened anyway? God alone can answer that. But were any of those prayers wasted or foolish or unneeded?

Is any prayer or walk ever that?

God Speed

THE WALKING LIVING

I have seen only two episodes of the show *The Walking Dead*.
People tell me I should have persevered, but I couldn't find
sufficient motivation for it. It's not that I don't find our obses-
sion with zombies interesting. Clearly, we're working out, as a
society, some deep-rooted anxieties about unstoppable incur-
able epidemics and unslakeable habits of consumption and
humans losing their humanity and tribalism and terrorism
and crazed hordes overrunning borders and much else that is
on our minds these days. A zombie apocalypse—that's just our
daily fears transmogrified, magnified, projected outward. And
turned into entertainment.

I get it. But it doesn't mean I have to sit and watch it.

What I did pick up from the two episodes I watched, and
also from the small handful of zombie movies I've seen (*I Am
Legend*, *World War Z*, *Pontypool*—a low budget Canadian flick
which, in my limited opinion, is the scariest of all) is that the
walking dead turn those who are still alive into no more than
survivors. They might be still living, still human, but barely.
No one flourishes. They all eke out an existence at the edge of
catastrophe. They fight over diminishing food supplies. They
lie. They grow paranoid. They distrust everyone. They exploit
one another. They become mean, wary, cruel, territorial.

Which all sounds eerily familiar. Maybe the zombie
apocalypse is already underway.

I am not, in general, a basher of "culture." I think that things now are both better and worse than things, say, twenty years ago or fifty or five hundred. We have raunchier movies but more vigilance over abuse. We have fewer sexual boundaries but less racism. It's safer to walk the streets of most major cities in the world today than it was in the eighties.

But some things are clearly on the slide. One of them is a sense of calm. We lack, more and more, evenhandedness and coolheadedness. We are, more and more, marked by fear and anxiety and irritation. We flare up more easily, break down more quickly, panic with little provocation, fume over minor complications. How could we even handle a zombie apocalypse when we flip out over sketchy wifi or rant on social media?

I have a solution to all this: we, you and I, become the Walking Living. We choose, because we can, to be signs of hope and grace. We don't melt down, flip out, fume, storm, gripe, rant. We choose kindness over irritation, every time. We do what Jesus sent his first disciples to do: speak peace wherever we go.

This is easy for those of us with a living hope. All we need is to stay in touch with that hope, and then live out of it.

I tried this today. I am writing this in a small town called Canmore, about forty minutes from the small town where I live, called Cochrane. I came here to work on this book. But I also decided that I needed every day, whatever the weather, to walk for at least an hour in and around the town. The first day, Cheryl was with me and we walked to the Grassi Lakes, two tiny but spectacular pools of the clearest water I've ever seen, with a bright laughing waterfall flowing between them. The second and third day, I was on my own and walked along the blue-green Elbow River, through a trail that connects with a boardwalk over muskeg and emerges at the edge of town. I looked around town both times, and bought a few groceries the second day, and then walked back by a different route.

I chose to be the Walking Living. I chose to greet all I passed and to chat with them if they seemed open and to be patient and kind to all. I chose to be a bright part of everyone's day. I chose to live out of my living hope.

Here's what I found: it's fun. And it self-generates and self-perpetuates: kindness begets kindness, hope begets hope, joy begets joy. Of course, surliness and greed and anger and fear do the same, self-generate and self-perpetuate.

Why not head out now? Everywhere you go, with everyone you meet, be the Walking Living.

CHAPTER 10

Walking as Attentiveness

Paris is one of the most walkable cities in the world. I've been there, so far, three times, and each time I've walked huge tracts of it: from Notre-Dame to the Eiffel Tower, from the Sacré-Coeur Basilica to the Louvre, from the Arc de Triomphe to the Bastille. I've strode long stretches of wide boulevards and meandered narrow twists of laneways.

I've walked myself weak-kneed and footsore, but deliriously happy.

On a recent trip with two friends, Kevin and Craig, we walked one day more than thirteen miles. This was, to be sure, partly from our cheapness: we looked into taking a boat down the Seine to get back to our apartment, but it cost more money than any of us wanted to pay, so we walked: six miles to save twelve euros. That seemed a fair exchange.

But mostly, we walked because Paris is magic, and walking is the best way to feel its enchantment. It's a city of a million small wonders, and several large ones. It bends and twists and rises and falls, and has approximately ten thousand bridges, give or take, each one beckoning you to cross, many bejeweled with those tokens of eternal love, metal locks, forever clasped, their keys tossed by lovers into the murky depths of the river below.[29] The city surprises at almost every turn. On nearly every corner, and all down each street, is a café to sit in for a minute, or an hour, and eat and drink something. Even the cheap wine is good. Even the weak coffee is strong. Even the stale croissants melt in your mouth. Even the nice waiters are a tad haughty.

What's not to adore?

This most recent trip, though, I noticed something else: the people living in Paris seem not the least enthralled by it. It is the place they live and work and buy groceries and wait in traffic. It is where they get stressed in their jobs and argue with their spouses and fret over their children. It's where they wonder how to make ends meet. They are, by all appearances, as bored and rushed and worried as most people most places. While tourists take pictures of the Eiffel Tower from every possible angle, gushing about its beauty, the locals push past, looking straight ahead, annoyed to have so many rubes and gawkers in their way. They never take even a single backward glance at what stuns and astonishes the rest of us.

Few who live in Paris, it seems, walk the city for pleasure. They walk it from necessity. They walk it to get from one place to the next.

I found that sad.

And then I found it familiar.

I live in a quaint small town next to the Rocky Mountains. I'm just down the road from the iconic Banff, and that is just down the road from the legendary Lake Louise. There's hardly a view around here that isn't jaw dropping. Grasslands and aspen forests roll out, in rising folds of green and gold, toward vast tracts of evergreens and, higher up, the towering granite and glaciated snow of the Rockies. A bending tumbling river, green as emerald, teeming with hungry feisty trout, cuts the middle of it. Moose and bear and wolf and badger and bighorn sheep roam the woods and fields, and sometimes venture into town.

But most days, I don't bother to look. I walk to the mailbox. I drive to work. I putter in the yard. Bored, rushed, worried. When I head to Banff, I usually wake up. But even so, I can get annoyed at the gawking tourists crowding the streets taking pictures—bedazzled, they are, by the knife-blade edge of Rundle Mountain, the wide arrowhead peak of Norquay Mountain, a herd of elk grazing, aloof and serene, in one of the local meadows. Travelers from all over the world point and exclaim. Me, I shuffle along, head down, muttering, shouldering past them.

I came back from my little epiphany in Paris and decided to notice things more. To slow down. To look up and look around. To see, to treasure, to savor. The beauty of this way of living is that, once you start, you notice how everything burns and hums and glows: not just the obvious spectacles but everything, every last little rock and twig and grass blade and dragonfly. The smallest leaf, held up against the sun, is a masterpiece of delicate intricate design, a piece of eternity so fine and perfect— and alive—that it's hard to think of a single manmade thing that rivals it. You can spend a week at the Louvre and barely cover it. But your back yard? That would take a lifetime.

But you could always start now.

THE SURPRISE OF THE FAMILIAR

That is one of the mysteries of walking: it keeps driving a place deeper into us and yet keeps opening up its secrets if we are attentive as we walk.

This is also true of walking with someone. The people I have gotten to know best are the people I have walked with. Walking is one of the primary ways that we become familiar with one another and yet also keep surprising each other. Recently, I walked half of Manhattan with my youngest daughter, Nicola. Afterward, our bodies ached—feet, shins, thighs. The next morning it was hard to move.[30] But the walking itself was revelatory. Walking immersed us in the spectacle of that great city. And as we walked, we reminisced, turning memories over and over, sometimes reminding one another of things the other had forgotten. We found out things about one another—histories, tastes, emotions, dreams—that we hadn't known before, or only vaguely. And we talked of the future.

I don't think all of that would have happened, or not nearly at the level it did, had we sat in our room and chatted or rode a cab together. Walking opens doors that sitting only strains against.

This is also true of walking with God. It deepens the familiar and yet keeps revealing the new.

BURIED TREASURE

Recently I heard theologian and author Belden Lane speak. Lane opened with a story about a poor and simple rabbi from Krakow, Poland, who dreams of a treasure hidden in faraway

Warsaw, a city he has never visited. But the dream is vivid. He sees the city, clear and distinct: the shape of its buildings, the layout of its streets, the sharpness of its rooflines. He sees in the center of the city a bridge—its arc, its span, its footings, the fast muddy water flowing beneath it. And he sees, under one footing of the bridge, a vast treasure buried there.

He dreams it night after night. He tells his wife the dream. She says he's crazy. But the dream is so real, so persistent, so insistent that he makes up his mind to walk to Warsaw and see for himself. It's a long way. As the city comes into view, he is astonished: the reality mirrors exactly his dream—the shape of the buildings, the layout of the streets, the sharpness of its rooflines. And there it is, the bridge, the river. Exactly. He finds his way down to where he knows treasure is buried.

But before he gets to it, a guard sees him, arrests him, detains him, interrogates him.

The poor and simple rabbi tells the truth. It's all he knows how to do.

The guard mocks him. "You stupid old man. Believing a dream! You know nothing of science. Nothing of how the world works. Why, these past two weeks, I have dreamed of a treasure buried under the cooking pot of a poor rabbi's home in Krakow. But I am too intelligent to travel all the way there for what I know does not exist."

The guard throws the rabbi out. The rabbi walks the long way back to his village. When he arrives home, he takes his cooking pot down, digs under the ash of the fire, finds a trapdoor in the floor panels, pries it open, and discovers a vast treasure. He lives into old age a wealthy man. The other villagers say this about him: though his treasure was always in Krakow, in his own village, in his own home, the knowledge of that treasure lay in Warsaw.

It is often a long walk to find what is right under our feet.

This is one of those made-up stories that is bone-deep true, a fable that is a parable of your life and mine. I have traveled many places and have beheld many strange and beautiful and sometimes heartrending things. Every journey, though, brings me home to discover, with fresh wonder and gratitude, the treasure under my own feet.

God Speed

A NEW THING

"See, I am doing a new thing!
Now it springs up; do you not perceive it?
I am making a way in the wilderness
and streams in the wasteland."

—ISAIAH 43:19

So says God through the prophet Isaiah. The context suggests the new thing is utmost surprise and stunning good news. And what must we do to receive it? Nothing . . . *except to perceive it.*

God's new thing is easy to miss, especially in the ordinary, familiar paths of life. This is the theme in most, maybe all, of Jesus' kingdom parables. The kingdom—God's new thing—always starts small, vanishingly small, so small that unless you're actually looking for it, you're not likely to see it.

The kingdom is a little seed. It's a stalk of grain among weeds. It's a priceless thing, a rare pearl, but at a quick glance it looks ordinary, small, unglamorous. It's hard to see, unless you're traveling God speed.

See, I'm doing a new thing! Do you not perceive it?

I once heard Eugene Peterson give a lecture about paying attention. He commented on the writing of Annie Dillard, particularly her work *Pilgrim at Tinker Creek*, a kind of Thoreau-esque meditation on living in one place deeply for a year. Peterson said he learned to see by reading Dillard. He said, and I'll try as best I can to distill his words, this: "Annie Dillard can write ten pages about going to the mailbox, and it's as riveting as someone else writing about climbing Everest or blazing a trail in the Amazon. She makes the ordinary exotic, thrilling, beautiful. I see the world around me better and clearer with her as my guide."[31]

How about a walk like that today? Pick a familiar route—maybe just to the mailbox. But look at it as though you're seeing it for the first time. Notice what you've never noticed, or at least notice some fresh detail. Then reflect on this question: What new thing might God be doing right now? What kingdom seed is waiting, buried with winter snows, or tentatively poking its head above the dirt?

Can I perceive it?

CHAPTER 11

Walking as Remembering

Cheryl and I returned last night from six weeks of travel. It involved some work, some play. We slept in twelve different beds in nine different cities, drove more than two thousand miles, flew almost seven thousand, sailed on eight different ferries, ate in more than thirty different restaurants, and read a bunch of books. I spoke seventeen times, Cheryl ten. I swam in the ocean only once, which is sad commentary on my old-man-ness: I was near, in view of, or right beside salt water for an entire month, but ventured in only once. (Not to confess someone else's sins, but Cheryl didn't swim in the ocean at all . . .) And we toured only two museums, also a sad commentary of sorts: we were in Mexico City for an entire week, a town that has, it seems, an art gallery or museum at every turn and corner.

I even ate a whole small octopus, served up with all eight legs splayed out pleadingly, suction cups puckering up at me, each leg curled up like a sad prayer, almost begging me to throw it back in the water.

But what stands out most over the entire six weeks was the

walking. We walked and walked and walked: sandy and pebbly beaches, rocky shorelines, forest trails, city parks, dirt roads, crowded streets, urban plazas.

We walked with my father-in-law, who is eighty-three and has late-stage Alzheimer's. He holds himself up with a push walker that has four wheels, hand brakes, and a little sling he can sit on if he gets pooped. Each time we went out, we set out from a home my mother- and father-in-law have lived in for sixty years. It's the home where Cheryl was first cradled and cooed over. We walked half a block up a gentle incline, stopped to rest, and then turned around and came back. The whole trip took half an hour.

I have been walking that particular neighborhood now for nigh on forty years, but those slow walks revealed things I'd never seen before: an exotic tree in a neighbor's yard, a weeping ghost of a thing, with branches thin as threads and leaves delicate as feathers, that seemed to be lamenting some unspeakable loss; an ugly gnomish lawn ornament with a pug-face scowl that must have been there for decades, it's so algae-coated and paint-chipped, but that startled me like a jack-in-the-box popping out two cranks too early; an alarmingly large crack working its way down the pavement, hinting at a seismic rift just waiting to yawn and swallow us whole.

These are things that reveal themselves only to a slow walker.

We walked about two miles in one area of Mexico City that felt, frankly, dangerous. We were two glaringly obvious tourists in a section of the city where tourists don't go, two rubes almost begging to be relieved of our cash and jewelry. And yet nothing happened, which makes me think, just perhaps, I was projecting a little. We also walked other parts of the same city, maybe ten miles in total, that felt friendly and safe and festive and beautiful, with stunning architecture, restaurants, green space, and public art installations.

We walked, on a small island, several miles up a narrow, bending gravel road that climbed through a thick coastal forest of cedars and spruce and Douglas fir and arbutus trees, with an understory of salal and ferns. Bald eagles cut wide gyres above. Views of tidal pools flickered through the foliage. One vehicle passed us the whole time.

We walked the downtown core of Vancouver, a city as glittery and radiant and, on a sunny day, drop-jaw gorgeous as a city can get, except for maybe those cities of the future imagined by dreamy utopians.

And much more.

Walking made it all magic. It opened perception and sealed memory. It combined sight and sound and smell and touch and taste. Some of those walks, even only days afterward, are already lost in a blur of forgetting, but several I can replay, top to bottom, with minutiae of detail, from the simplest cue: I think Lasqueti Island and feel, once more, the roundness and looseness of small colorful stones beneath my feet in Spring Bay or smell the forest's perfume of sea salt and cedar boughs; I see the pink side of the hop-on-hop-off bus in Mexico City and smell again meat roasting in the cathedral square or hear afresh that street band across from the National Museum nail a cover of "You Really Got Me." I picture the Japanese garden on that warm July evening in Kelowna and hear again the thrum of hummingbird wings or taste anew the sweet burst of fresh-picked cherries.

Walking is a memory boost. Alan Castel, in *Psychology Today*, writes, "People want to know how they can improve their memory. Computer-based 'brain-training'? Doing crossword puzzles? Eating blueberries? The one method that has strong evidence-based support is simple: walking."[32]

Robyn Davidson attests to this. In her book *Tracks*, about her solo trek across 1,700 miles of Australian desert, she documents the almost supernatural powers of recall that walking, and solitude, had on her:

> Strange things do happen when you trudge twenty miles a day, day after day, month after month. Things you only become totally conscious of in retrospect. For one thing I had remembered in minute and technicolour detail everything that has ever happened in my past and all the people who belong there. And I had remembered every word of conversation I had had or overheard way, way back in my childhood, and in this way I have been able to review these events with a kind of emotional detachment as if they had happened to somebody else. I was rediscovering and getting to know people who are long since dead and forgotten. . . . And I was happy, there is simply no other word for it.[33]

PETER'S MEMORY PALACE

Tradition says that the apostle Peter narrated the events behind the gospel of Mark. That sounds right—not least because Peter comes off slapstick, tongue-tied, bumbling in that gospel, and it's hard to imagine Mark risking such a portrait of the chief apostle except with the expressed permission, and even fixed insistence, of the man himself.

Many things leap out from the story: Jesus' secretiveness about his identity, his urgency about his mission, his fierce authority and equally fierce compassion, his power and his humility all bound up together. But one thing is most striking: how much Jesus and his crew walk. I've already noticed this in chapter 7, but I want to comment on it here in light of this chapter's theme about walking and memory. I wonder if Peter's recollection of what Jesus did and said was attached to their travel itinerary. I wonder, in other words, whether walking became Peter's memory palace: the itinerary itself served as the mental architecture for Peter to store and retrieve each event. *Okay, that day we landed in Bethsaida, Jesus spit—twice!—in that blind man's eyes, and then we bombed up to Caesarea Philippi and Jesus asked us who people said he was, and then he asked us each the same thing personally, and then Jesus started talking about his death, and then John and James and I went up that mountain with him and saw him all dazzling white . . .*

Of course, all these events are unforgettable in and of themselves. But the whole trip, all three years of it, was a whirlwind—blasting demons, healing lepers, rebutting Pharisees, catering meals for huge crowds—and if Peter was anything like me, then he would have tended to get details muddled. I'm guessing that what helped keep everything straight is he remembered where he walked, and his remembering each journey pulled along with it everything else: faces, names, expressions, conversations, emotions.

The texture of each moment was tied to the footfall of each journey.

ALWAYS REMEMBER, NEVER FORGET

The biblical event that links most closely walking with remembering is the exodus, the journey Israel took to get out of Egypt and into Canaan. It was a trip that should have taken about two weeks, give or take. But it took forty years, give or take. The Israelites needed the extra time to get themselves properly sorted out.

The exodus is as much about remembering as anticipating. It is about the past as much as the future. Maybe more so. The Israelites walk and walk and walk, on hot sand, under burning sky, eating the same meal day in, day out. They walk toward promised land, but also away from captivity. They get ready, with each stride, for what is coming. But they also remember, with each step, what has been. "Those who forget the past," philosopher George Santayana said, "are doomed to repeat it." But it's no new insight: God says this repeatedly, and has for a long while. Moses, God's friend and servant, is one of God's main mouthpieces for this truth.

Moses' strongest call to remember arrives at the end of the exodus event—strongest, that is, exactly at the moment when everyone's temptation to forget would be at its peak, when the euphoria of "we're almost there" would have been a kind of delirium. Moses, ancient, bent with age, looks toward a land he himself will never enter and speaks his final words to the people he's traveled and travailed with for forty years. It's a sermon, actually. It's a sermon, like most sermons, that mixes instruction with warning, theology with advice. Mostly, though, it's a sermon about remembering:

> Remember the day you stood before the LORD your God at Horeb. . . . Remember that you were slaves in Egypt and that the LORD your God brought you out of there with a mighty hand and an outstretched arm. . . . Remember well what the

LORD your God did to Pharaoh and to all Egypt.... Remember how the LORD your God led you all the way in the wilderness these forty years. . . . Remember the LORD your God, for it is he who gives you the ability to produce wealth. . . . Remember this and never forget how you aroused the anger of the LORD your God in the wilderness. . . . Remember the days of old; consider the generations long past.

—DEUTERONOMY 4:10; 5:15; 7:18; 8:2, 18; 9:7;
32:7; AND THERE ARE SEVERAL MORE

And so on, and so on. There's a lot to remember: where you've been, who you've been, how you got from there to here. Above all, it's a sermon about remembering God, our God, the God who keeps rescuing and healing and disciplining and leading us, the God who's been with us all the way down, all the way through. To the very ends of the age.

You'll soon be leaving the barren wasteland you've been wandering around in half your life, dodging snakes, gnawing quail, trying to swallow another bite of manna without tasting it. You'll soon walk over a border into a good land flowing with milk and honey. Kind of like Canada. After a bit of a dustup in Jericho, a few scuffles here and there with giants and people whose last names all end in *ite*, you'll settle—pastures, houses, barns, fat dairy cows, a swing set for the kids, a two-door refrigerator plus a freezer chest in the garage, and much more—and grow fat yourself on all that milk and honey.

And you will stop walking, more or less. That's the thing about settling: it's the opposite of moving. There are many upsides to this, so obvious there's no use naming any. But there are a few downsides too: sitting around is not the best regimen for your heart, physical or otherwise. Comfort tends to breed forgetfulness, and forgetfulness complacency, and complacency arrogance, and arrogance entitlement.

This, in fact, is one of Moses' biggest warnings:

> Remember how the LORD your God led you all the way in the wilderness these forty years. . . . For the LORD your God is bringing you into a good land—a land with brooks, streams, and deep springs gushing out into the valleys and hills; a land with wheat and barley, vines and fig trees, pomegranates, olive oil and honey; a land where bread will not be scarce and you will lack nothing; a land where the rocks are iron and you can dig copper out of the hills.
>
> When you have eaten and are satisfied, praise the LORD your God for the good land he has given you. Be careful that you do not forget the LORD your God. . . . Otherwise, when you eat and are satisfied, when you build fine houses and settle down, and when . . . all you have is multiplied, then your heart will become proud and you will forget the LORD your God.

—DEUTERONOMY 8:2, 7–14

When you eat and are satisfied, when you build fine houses and settle down, and when all you have is multiplied, then your heart . . .

I live in Canaan, or Canada—hard sometimes to tell the two apart—and I get, intimately, this little chain of logic: *when, when, when, then.* I know deep down all the ways the *when* of blessing plays havoc with the *then* of my heart. It tends to work opposite of how it should: I become entitled rather than thankful, smug rather than humble, hoarding rather than generous, imperious rather than kind. A tyrant, not a servant.

Oh, you too?

But here's something I never noticed before now: the danger comes with *settling*. It's when people stop their walking that they become most susceptible to forgetting. It's idleness that makes them, and us, most susceptible to that little damning logic chain of *when, when, when, then*.

The Israelites, of course, were not always model citizens in the wilderness, in their wanderings. They grumbled, a lot. They made idols out of earrings. They plotted mutiny. They had orgies. There's Moses, tempted to call down a drone strike on all their pointy little heads.

But even so, when the people were on foot they never seemed far from remembering. Wandering seemed the perfect recipe for bringing it all back to mind—God's nearness and goodness, his bounty and love. They always only ever seemed a *step* away from remembering the story whole: once we were not a people, but now we are the people of God. Once we were slaves in Egypt. Now we are a royal priesthood, headed to a good place.

Walking is a good goad for remembering. Every time we break camp, strike out, put one leg in front of the next, it helps us recall the God who has been with us all the way down, all the way through.

God Speed

MEMORY LANE

Recently, Cheryl and I spoke at a family camp. We were thinking a lot about this book and decided to try out some of its ideas. So, besides each of us giving a number of talks, we also got people walking, every day. The first day we talked about calling and identity, and then got them walking alone, listening to God. The second day we talked about friendship, and then got them walking with one other person they knew well. The third day we talked about personal mission, and then had them walk with someone they didn't know. The fourth and last day, we talked about participating in Jesus' mission, and then had them walk in groups, six groups altogether, and compose a psalm that gathered and expressed all they had experienced over the week.

The results stunned us. All six groups wrote thoughtful and beautiful psalms, some they performed as songs, each capturing what happened: couples falling in love again, a man finding fresh hope in a dark season, a woman hearing God for the first time, many people letting go of bitterness and fear and anger. I imagine some of this would have happened anyway, even if all Cheryl and I did all week was stand and talk, and all the rest did was sit and listen. But I think the vividness and concreteness of our experience, individually, collectively, its fine-textured particularity, might have been dulled if we'd only talked while others listened. Walking, if nothing else, enhanced memory, and in some instances, I think, released it.

It's worth a try. In your next walk, just walk. Pay the normal amount of attention you would any other time. If you're walking for exercise or companionship or to get somewhere, walk as you always do. Don't strain for effect. Don't try to store up anything.

Just walk.

But afterward—say, several hours after or even a day or two—see how much you remember, not just about the walk but about what you saw and said and heard and thought and felt. And see how much you remembered all the ways God has met you and blessed you.

Write it down. See if you find that walking enhances memory and maybe even releases it.

PRESSING ON

Not that I have already obtained all this,
or have already arrived at my goal, but
I press on to take hold of that for which
Christ Jesus took hold of me.

—PHILIPPIANS 3:12

CHAPTER 12

Walking as Suffering

A few years ago, driving in Italy with my wife and two daughters, I took a wrong turn. We had spent the morning visiting the ruins of Pompeii, that city encased in the eternal now. On August 24, AD 79, the nearby volcano of Vesuvius exploded and dropped fifteen feet of volcanic ash on the place. Boys running down streets, women laundering clothes, men haggling over produce, horses pulling carts—all were caught midflight and turned to stone.

Driving away, thinking of mortality and of the questionable immortality of turning to stone, I went wrong. I turned right instead of left, west instead of east. At first, no big deal. I could see the highway I was supposed to be on, running parallel with the highway I was actually on. There will be, I figured, a juncture soon, and the two will become one.

But no. A few miles down the road, the two split asunder, never to rejoin. Well, that's not quite true: they do rejoin, but a mountain lies between them. I could not reckon how to turn myself around, and all the other drivers (this was southern Italy, after all) were racing each other like charioteers in a reenact-ment of *Ben-Hur*. I kept missing exits. Plus I don't read or speak Italian, so all the signage merely taunted me.

And so I ended up driving, with my wife and two daughters, the entire length of the Amalfi Coast.

The Amalfi Coast is, end to end, breathtakingly beautiful.

The Amalfi Coast is, end to end, heart-stoppingly terrifying.

It is all of thirty miles, but takes nearly three hours to drive. The alternate route, on the other side of the mountain, takes thirty minutes.

Why the difference? The inland route is a straight shot up and over a mountain pass: short, wide, quick, cheap. (Well, not cheap: there's a toll. My advice: pay it, and be happy you did.)

Above all, it is safe.

The coastal route is as coiled as a snake, bent as a corkscrew, thin as a blade. It is so narrow you have to flip your sideview mirror to avoid knocking oncoming vehicles, most of which are buses or semis. But the best, and worst, part: it is high as a bird, soaring one thousand feet above the Tyrrhenian Sea, which glit-ters blue and green far below and straight down. One bad turn, you plummet all the way, with enough time in the descent to fully contemplate your mistake.

It is the hard way and narrow way.

I generally like driving. But three hours on the Amalfi Coast—beautiful as it is—took me three days to recover from: to unravel my knotted muscles, unlock my gritted teeth, pry loose my death grip. It took that long to get color back into my bone-white knuckles and breath into my parched lungs and stillness into my thundering heart.

Would I do it again?

Right now, if I could.

Which is the irony of hard ways: they are, at the very least, memorable. Once in a while, they change your life.

My bent, maybe yours, is to find the easy way every time: the shortest distance, the widest path, the quickest route, the cheapest means, the safest course. Everything in me craves that. Yet the times I've stumbled upon the hard way—the long stretch, the costly journey, the twisted path, the route that doubles back, circles round, crisscrosses, detours, skirts the precipice—those have been the best.

The way of suffering is often the way of revelation.

NO STRAIGHT PATH

I tried to map Jesus' walks in the gospel of Mark. He is a blur of coming and going. The Lord of the Sabbath, the Prince of Peace is in an all-fired-up rush. First-century peasant footwear in Israel, the Tanakhi sandal, was flimsy: a slab of untreated leather laced to foot and ankle by grass or leather thongs. They wore out quickly. Jesus, saving souls from burning, would have burned through a lot of soles tramping Palestine's hot, rough, stony roadways and pathways.

What's especially striking is how scattershot his itinerary is: he circuits around Galilee, then hightails it over to Lebanon, then circles back to Galilee, then thunders up to the Golan Heights, then sails over to Syria, and much else. A bit of route planning would have spared him a lot of miles and blisters.

But I think this was his plan. All his back-and-forth, all his here and there, accomplished at least two things. One, it allowed him more time to walk and talk with his disciples, and Mark's gospel in particular suggests they needed this: they were slow on the uptake, often thick as posts. And two, it demonstrated something at the core of discipleship: there is no straight path. There is no easy way. There is no quick, no fast, no wide, no cheap, no safe.

Ironically, one of Mark's favorite words is *straightway*. He uses it more than forty times, though most translations render it as *immediately* or *at once* or *as soon as*. Some translations bury it almost entirely, treat it as a verbal tic. But Mark uses that word, *straightway*, at nearly every turn: "*Straightway* he saw the heavens being torn open. . . . The Spirit *straightway* drove him out into the wilderness. . . . *Straightway* they left their nets and followed him. . . . *Straightway* he called them. . . . *Straightway* on the Sabbath he entered the synagogue. . . . *Straightway* there was in their synagogue a man with an unclean spirit. . . . *Straightway* he left the synagogue and entered the house. . . . *Straightway* they told him. . . . *Straightway* the leprosy left him."

That's just the first chapter.

And yet Jesus' straightway isn't straight.

This is true also about following Jesus. Those who want things convenient, who want them straightway—in Mark, as in the other gospels, this is mostly religious people, but also disciples—are often disappointed. With religious people, when Jesus doesn't puzzle them, he enrages them. When they're not arguing with him, they're plotting against him. The kind of people who should know better rarely do. But the kind of people who shouldn't know better—prostitutes, tax collectors, sundry sinners, uneducated folk, and suchlike—they are the ones who make straightway to Jesus, though we can imagine their journey up until the last leg has been anything but straight.

But Jesus himself does not choose the straightway. He wanders highways and byways. He seeks out lonely places. He rambles about in the wilderness. He plots the longest distance between two points and takes that. Given a choice between a safe quick route and a slow dangerous one, he almost always picks the latter.

He almost always picks the way of suffering. The *via dolorosa*.

THE HARD WAY

Many Christians—many people, in fact—have grasped, maybe not consciously but at least instinctively, a basic life principle: the hard way usually forms us more deeply and lastingly than any shortcut, any easy route, any road that's well lit and pounded flat. The easy route rarely transforms anyone.

I'm thinking of a friend I'll call Michael. He is someone I would trust with my treasures, my secrets, my dreams, my griefs. It wasn't always so. There was a time I thought him cocky. (Looking back, I see now that his cockiness mirrored my own and, frankly, threatened it.) He's tall, handsome, smart. He knew it and carried it all like a chest of medals, like it was all stuff he earned.

But then his life fell apart, and kept falling apart. It was a long road of heartache. Loss, failure, betrayal—all this and much else fell on him like pillagers, ambushed him like bandits. He kept walking. It only got worse.

But it made him better. Not all at once, and not all the time. There were days, there were weeks, there were months, when he raged and wept and entertained dark thoughts. He felt the futility of it all. His hopes stained dark. His prayers turned to dust. His heart hardened to stone. But gradually, slowly, step by blistering step, all that pain did its terrible holy work. It scoured him clean. It winnowed him pure. It made him a saint.

He still has days when it hurts all over. When he wants nothing more than not to get out of bed. Or to finish the day by finishing off a bottle of wine, all by himself. But mostly, he is kind and wise and humble. He's generous. He's a friend of sinners. If I had to sum up Michael in a word, it would be grace. He's drenched with it. It spills from him, in speech, in act, in manner. You see it in his eyes, hear it in his voice. An hour with Michael is a long soak in healing waters.

All this is the gift of the *via dolorosa*, the way of suffering.

A BITTER OLD WOMAN

Consider the story of Naomi, told in the book of Ruth. Naomi and her husband, Elimelech, and their two sons, Mahlon and Kilion, live in Bethlehem. Bethlehem means "house of bread." But it's down to crumbs and crusts for them: famine stalks the land, strips it bare and dry, bleaches it white. The ground demands more sweat and toil than their withering strength can muster and gives nothing in return. Harvests wilt even as they sprout.

They move to Moab. Moab is a historic enemy, and besides which their national god—Moloch or Milcom or Malcam, who might also be Chemosh, the destroyer—has a nasty habit: he devours children. At the heart of Moabite worship is child sacrifice. You want to flourish? It will cost you, dearly. It will cost you what you love the most.

Moab represents everything people like Elimelech and

Naomi have spent their entire lives detesting, denouncing, avoiding. And now they're here.

But soon after, Elimelech dies, we know not how. Let's imagine his old heart gave out.

Mahlon and Kilion marry Moabite girls, Orpah and Ruth. We're not sure who marries which, but likely Mahlon marries Orpah; Kilion, Ruth. Either way, it's a heartache for Naomi: she's dreamed since the boys were knee-high to a locust that each would find a good stout Israelite girl to grind and knead his flour into bread, and to make babies with. Instead, the boys pick foreign girls, women whose god might one day demand their babies.

And then, abruptly, both boys die, we know not how. Let's imagine their young bodies gave out.

Naomi is bitter. So bitter, she now calls herself that: Bitter, Mara. And she knows exactly who's to blame, who to blame, who's devoured her life, her loved ones, her children: it's God, he's the culprit. The God she grew up worshiping. She gave herself to God wholly, and he gave her nothing in return. Indeed, he took from her what she loved the most. "Don't call me Naomi. . . . Call me Mara, because the Almighty has made my life very bitter. I went away full, but the LORD has brought me back empty. Why call me Naomi? The LORD has afflicted me; the Almighty has brought misfortune upon me" (Ruth 1:20–21).

A rumor reaches Naomi's windburned ears: Bethlehem is once again living up to its name. There is bread to spare in her father's house. She makes plans to return. At first, her two daughters-in-law appear to go with her, but Naomi turns to them as they set out on the road and tells them to go back, back to their homes, back to their people, back to their gods. Go, go, find Moabite boys to marry and make bread for and babies with. Orpah, with much emotion, takes her up on this.

But Ruth will have none of it. "Where you go I will go, and where you stay I will stay. Your people will be my people and your God my God. Where you die I will die, and there I will be buried" (vv. 16–17).

And so the two women, one bitter beyond measure, one loyal beyond reckoning, begin the long way back to the House of Bread.

Why does Ruth follow this bitter old woman? Why is she loyal, unto death, to this Mara who openly blames God for all of her heartache? Where is the witness, the winsomeness, in Naomi's rage and sourness?

Likely, Ruth has seen Naomi at her best—her most resilient, most determined, most pleasant (the meaning of the name Naomi)—so that now, when Ruth sees Naomi at her worst, she knows it's not the whole story. I hope that people do not take my worst moments for the whole story.

But there's something else going on here. Naomi holds nothing back from her God. She blasts God with the full weight of her anger and misery. She pounds her fists against God's chest. She yells in his face. She lays all the blame at his feet.

Ruth could never do that with Moloch.

Try it: Go to the god who demands you sacrifice your children to feed his hungry maw and tell him you're not happy with the service. That he's brutal and you're bitter and you'd like to speak with the manager. Moloch doesn't care. Not even a little. He is not the kind of god prone to put up with your personal grievances. He just stokes the fire in his belly, snarls, and demands more.

Ruth grew up with that. Now she watches Naomi *kvetch*—no better word for it—and she glimpses something wondrously strange and beautiful: Naomi's God can handle her deepest pain, even as she blames him for it. *Naomi complains to God about God.* No one outside Israel has ever seen this before. No other faith, ever, anywhere, is like this, that you can complain to God about God. No other God, ever, anywhere, has acted this way, that he will take the fall for things gone tragically awry. No other God, ever, anywhere, welcomes us to lay the yoke of our sorrow and bitterness on his shoulders and drive the nails of our grievances through his flesh.

No wonder, then, that Ruth will follow Naomi anywhere. No wonder Ruth wants Naomi's God as her own. No wonder.

In time, the two women arrive in Bethlehem.

And everything turns around. But it's slow, slow, as these things tend to be. Ruth finds a less-than-minimum-wage job as a gleaner. It's hand-to-mouth kind of work. It's bending and straightening, all the day long. It puts food on the table, barely.

But the landowner, Boaz, takes a shine to Ruth. And things start to happen—some the fruit of human plotting, some the outcome of a hidden providence—and soon Ruth and Boaz marry, and soon she is with child. It's a son. They call him Obed.

The women of Bethlehem say that Obed is not Ruth's son but Naomi's. That feels right: Ruth conceives and bears and gives birth to Obed, but it's Naomi (who somewhere along the line has let go of the name Mara) whose emptiness is now fullness.

Actually, it's more than that. Obed is, in a sense, now everyone's son. The book of Ruth ends with a genealogy, and the last bit of that is this: "Boaz [was] the father of Obed, Obed the father of Jesse, and Jesse the father of David" (4:21–22).

Which ties in with another genealogy: "Boaz the father of Obed, *whose mother was Ruth*, Obed the father of Jesse, and Jesse the father of King David" (Matt 1:5–6, emphasis mine).

And then twenty-seven generations follow, ending here: "And Jacob the father of Joseph, the husband of Mary, and Mary was the mother of Jesus who is called the Messiah" (v. 16).

That's a long hard road to a good place. That's a way of suffering to a house of bread, and bread to spare.

WHERE NOW?

So should we seek the hard way, the way of suffering? Should we spurn all roads but this one?

No. That's called masochism.

But should we welcome it? Should we choose this road, make it our own, when there is no other?

Yes. That's called wisdom.

There's a holy paradox here. There is no gain in chasing pain. But there is often much gain in bearing it. Pain is a poor guru but a rich tutor. It's not the teacher you seek, not ever. But it's the teacher who sometimes shows up, unbidden. Heed her. She'll teach you things and form you in ways that all the ease in the world knows not even rumors of.

God Speed

THE *VIA DOLOROSA*

Latin has several words that English swallowed whole. English took them into its own wide belly and passed them out again undigested: they mean the same, sound the same, are spelled the same as the day we found them. Other Latin words we spat out like bones. We tossed away perfectly fine phrases like *vero nihil verius* (nothing truer than truth) or *caelum non animum mutant qui trans mare currunt* (those who rush across the sea change the sky, but not their souls). But we kept intact *bona fide, carpe diem, caveat emptor, de facto, et cetera, vice versa, veto.*

And this: *via.* The way.

Jesus' last walk before his death was in Jerusalem between the Praetorium, where Roman soldiers beat him, and Golgotha, where Roman soldiers killed him.[34] We call this route the *Via Dolorosa*: the way of suffering. It is twisting but short—less than half a mile.

Every step would have been searing pain. Uphill. His back bleeding from a scourging with leather thongs, each laced with metal shards and bone chips, cracked thirty-nine times across his back, his legs, his sides. His head bleeding from fists and thorns. Staggering beneath a hundred pounds of rough-hewn timber,[35] stretched out on wounded shoulders, until finally he had no strength to carry it farther. And many who watched, hurling insults.

Besides his physical agony, Jesus walked to his own

death knowing that he would be killed by crucifixion, maybe the most brutal and prolonged means of lethal torture ever devised. The pain was just beginning. And he knew that he was being killed for a crime he did not commit.

And there was a third thing he knew: God wanted this. God willed it. "Yet it was the LORD's will to crush him and cause him to suffer" (Isa. 53:10).

Jesus knew, and we know, his death was a ransom for us. He knew, and we know, that

> he was pierced for our transgressions,
>> he was crushed for our iniquities;
> the punishment that brought us peace was on him,
>> and by his wounds we are healed.
> We all, like sheep, have gone astray,
>> each of us has turned to our own way;
> and the LORD has laid on him
>> the iniquity of us all.

—ISAIAH 53:5–6

And we know that "for the joy set before him he endured the cross, scorning its shame, and sat down at the right hand of the throne of God" (Heb. 12:2).

But all that knowing did not lighten the sorrow or remove the pain. The lashes still cut deep into flesh. The crossbeam still bent his body double and turned his legs to mush. The insults still struck his heart. The nails still pierced his skin and bone and muscle. They still sheared nerves.

The *via dolorosa.*

Christians for centuries have walked the traditional route in Jerusalem, trying to imagine Christ's agony, seeking to experience afresh, at its source, the power of Christ's sacrifice. But even more so, Christians for centuries have found in Christ's last walk a point of solidarity with their own pain. It has helped them make sense of their suffering and grief and loss. It has been a way of knowing "the fellowship of His sufferings, becoming conformed to His death" (Phil. 3:10 NKJV).

But this is also the way of knowing "the power of his resurrection" and somehow to attain our own "resurrection from the dead" (vv. 10–11 NIV). The *via dolorosa* is, strangely, beautifully, also the *via et resurrectionis erimus*—the way of resurrection.

That's what those who have walked in solidarity with Christ's sorrow have often found: that as we bring our sufferings into communion with Christ's sufferings, we join our sorrow to his sorrow, our loss to his loss, our pain to his pain, and together we walk to the place of death. But we also walk past it, to the place of new life. We go from the *via dolorosa* to the *via et resurrectionis erimus.*

My typical way of dealing with pain is to deny it or avoid it or, when those methods fail, deal with it in as fast and superficial a way as possible. But a number of years ago I went through a time of deep and prolonged soul suffering, and none of that worked. And so I walked, a lot. I walked and cried and cried out, and sometimes raged. I felt Jesus beside me, step for step. I felt that there was nothing I suffered that he didn't know already, and intimately. *A man of sorrows, familiar with suffering. A high priest who empathizes with my weakness* (Heb. 4:15).

Those walks were slow and long and mostly silent. Jesus rarely spoke during them. But he listened. And once in a while, he turned his sad heavy head toward me and looked me straight in the eyes, and that was all I needed.

It took months. But little by little, we came to the place of the skull. The place of death. We stood together and looked at it a long time, and I felt, and felt that he felt, all the terrible sorrow of that place.

And then, amazingly, Jesus kept walking. I kept walking with him. We walked, together, right through the tomb into daylight.

Do you need to find your own *Via Dolorosa?* Is there pain in your life that no amount of ignoring or running from can banish? Pain that, unless you walk it all the way to the end, you will never get past?

You have a good companion. He knows the way. Maybe today is a good day to start.

CHAPTER 13

Walking as Healing

Jacob limps.

Look at him, walking with broken steps toward his brother, Esau. The rising sun, already laced with fire, is a bloody halo behind his head. He hobbles. He lurches. His good leg has to compensate for his bad one, almost to drag it. He hauls the bad leg up like he's pulling a body from a pit, and then brings it down hard and jarring, like he's throwing the body back in. He winces with the effort, with the aching. Maybe—maybe—Esau has pity on him at that moment, watching his younger brother struggle, watching his body stagger and lurch. Maybe that's when Esau's anger turns to kindness, and he runs—runs: such good legs he has!—to Jacob, and kisses him, embraces him, welcomes him, instead of doing what he'd threatened years before: killing him (Gen. 33:1–4).

Well, maybe.

I've never limped. Unless you count the time I tore the inside of my thigh playing hockey and could barely drive, let alone walk, for two weeks. Or the time I took that spill skiing and spent a month nursing a banged-up knee. Or the time I had that mysterious twinge in my shin that showed up for no apparent reason and went away without one either, but in the meantime played havoc with my walking.

But those are exceptions that prove the rule: I've never limped.

Also, I've always limped.

I've limped the same way Jacob limped before it became physical, before he spent a long sweaty night wrestling with and wresting things from God—a new name, a blessing (Gen. 32:22–32). After that face-to-face with God, Jacob never walked straight again. Or maybe he never walked crooked again. Maybe he limped but for the first time walked the line.

What we do know is that Jacob was crooked from the womb. And that's where he's my kin. Maybe your kin too? Since birth, I've had a flaw that's made me crooked. And even all my wrestling with God, wresting things from God, has not healed it whole.

But I keep walking. And limping.

It seems to be doing some good. It's just slow. About three-miles-an-hour slow. God speed.

THE WALKING CURE

In all my fifty-nine years, only once has a doctor told me I should, as much as possible, avoid walking. That was because he couldn't diagnose what was wrong with my aching leg and thought walking would make it worse. I ignored him and walked anyhow, and the leg got better.

Every other time that I've had an injury that impeded

walking, part of my doctor's prescribed cure was to walk. Not run. Not skip. Not jump. Not ski or play hockey or kickbox or even ride a bike.

But walk.

Sigmund Freud spoke about the talking cure—that a person's neurosis often got better simply by talking about it. But the walking cure is, I think, as effective, maybe more so. Walking is almost always part of any therapy. Depression. Grief. Obesity. Congestive heart failure. Bodily injury. Walk it out. Walk it off.

St. Augustine: *Solvitur ambulando.* "It is solved by walking."

Limping gets better by walking.

When my brother, quite recently, had a heart transplant, the nurses had him up and out of bed within a few days, urging him to walk. The surgical cut on his chest was a bright red gash. He wore an oxygen mask. He was medicated into ethereal bliss. His naked butt hung out his cotton gown. But they forced him from his bed and made him walk. In his initial trip, he merely shuffled from bed to doorway and back again. But they were relentless, day and night, and soon he was managing long stretches of hallway, and then laps around the floor, and then stairs. Before long, he was skedaddling through the ward and then the entire building, footloose and fancy free. A man about town. A Parisian *flaneur*, walking his turtle. Or at least his stuffed turtle.

It is solved by walking. It is healed by walking. More often than not, walking is part of how we get better.

My father was diagnosed late in life with type-2 diabetes. He had abused his body early in life with hard liquor and smoking, and after he quit those, with food and sedentariness. He drove everywhere. He watched inordinate amounts of television. He ate too much, and mostly the wrong things. He never exercised. He was forty pounds overweight and idle as a lap cat. Then he got a bad medical report.

It startled him into instant reform. He changed his whole lifestyle overnight. He ate well. He stopped watching television almost entirely. And he walked—not just around the block a time or two but like the great poets and philosophers once walked, over rugged terrain, in all kinds of weather, for miles and miles, every day.

He lost all the extra weight and never gained it back. He recovered a love of life. He laughed with genuine mirth, at nothing, at everything, like children do. His long wearying battle with anger gave way to quietness, to tenderness.

He still died too young, at sixty-seven, from a massive heart attack that had been stalking him for years. But he died happy. He died full of years—deeply alive, with a carefreeness I'd never seen in him before, not angry and sad and stuck like he'd been for decades. Obviously, better eating had something to do with this. But as I watched him get thin, get whole, come alive, the one thing I'm sure made the greatest difference was walking. It slowed him down and took him far. He discovered the walking cure. "We are eternally perplexed by how to move toward forgiveness or healing or truth," Rebecca Solnit writes, "but we know how to walk from here to there, however arduous the journey."[36]

He was not a man of faith, my father, at least not that he let on. He spoke dismissively, sometimes mockingly, about the church and Christians' "naive" beliefs. But he also had a weakness for watching Billy Graham, and late in his life he began to speak of Jesus with grudging admiration, even flickering affection. Yet he never openly professed faith. So I don't know if he ever thought about God or spoke to God on those long walks. Most of them were solitary, except for his dog, who joyfully overcame his own injuries to companion with him. The few times I joined him, we walked mostly in silence.

But I think God walked with him. And I think, sometimes, my father was aware of that and didn't mind. I like to picture the two of them, my father, the Father, silent, pensive, attentive, slow. Keeping pace with one another. God speed. Listening, listening to everything: the whir of insects in the grasses, the sniffing and shambling of the dog, the clack of gravel underfoot, the call of birds, the thrum of distant traffic, the deep hum of creation. And listening, too, to each other's breath, that deep exchange of inside and outside, the circling movements of *pneuma*.

I don't know. This is maybe only a son's sentimental wish.

What I do know is that my father's healing came from walking, by becoming pedestrian, and I think God was somehow involved with that. I think God made things this way, that walking is often the way we heal: it's not much of a stretch, then, to imagine that God draws near to those who walk. Who move at God speed.

GET UP AND WALK!

Among the many healing stories in the Gospels, only two have to do directly with walking. There's the story of the paralyzed man, told thrice, and variously, once each in Matthew, Mark, and Luke; and there's the story told only by John, the man at the pool of Bethesda. Mark and Luke add to the first story, the one about the paralyzed man, the detail that his friends make a hole in the roof and lower the man, bed and all, down through it.

(One scholar speculates that it was Jesus' own home whose roof they were pulling apart, though most think it was Peter's; if it was Jesus' home, the healing comes at the cost of damaging his living quarters[37]—an idea that fits well with the character of Jesus.)

It's the story in John, though, the one about the man at the pool of Bethesda, that especially captures me.

> Some time later, Jesus went up to Jerusalem for one of the Jewish festivals. Now there is in Jerusalem near the Sheep Gate a pool, which in Aramaic is called Bethesda and which is surrounded by five covered colonnades. Here a great number of disabled people used to lie—the blind, the lame, the paralyzed. One who was there had been an invalid for thirty-eight years. When Jesus saw him lying there and learned that he had been in this condition for a long time, he asked him, "Do you want to get well?"
>
> "Sir," the invalid replied, "I have no one to help me into the pool when the water is stirred. While I am trying to get in, someone else goes down ahead of me."
>
> Then Jesus said to him, "Get up! Pick up your mat and walk." At once the man was cured; he picked up his mat and walked.
>
> The day on which this took place was a Sabbath, and so the Jewish leaders said to the man who had been healed, "It is the Sabbath; the law forbids you to carry your mat."
>
> But he replied, "The man who made me well said to me, 'Pick up your mat and walk.'"
>
> So they asked him, "Who is this fellow who told you to pick it up and walk?"

The man who was healed had no idea who it was, for Jesus had slipped away into the crowd that was there.

Later Jesus found him at the temple and said to him, "See, you are well again. Stop sinning or something worse may happen to you." The man went away and told the Jewish leaders that it was Jesus who had made him well.

—JOHN 5:1–15

Thirty-eight years. That's a lifetime. This man languished away his childhood in dark rooms. He strained to listen, I would guess, to sounds of other children playing in the streets, or strained maybe not to hear it. He spent years watching shadows shuttle across the cracks at the bottom of doors. No one ever came to sit with him. As he aged, his body itched and burned with bed rashes. His limbs withered, his skin hung. Blood clots swelled his legs. He ached all over, except in the places he'd gone numb.

Maybe for a time his condition, fixed in one place as he was, loosed his imagination. Maybe his inner world soared. In his mind, he could go anywhere—Spain, towering mountains, wide-open plains. He could be anything—warrior, sailor, prince. Carpenter. Bricklayer. Maybe he dreamed of flying, of plundering, of lovemaking. Of cutting his own bread that his own hands had earned.

But now he's thirty-eight, or older, and his imagination has narrowed to one thing: the fading hope that today, for some reason, when that miasmic slew of water churns in the pool behind his head, someone will happen by, will have pity on him, on him alone. They will lift his frail body, carry him to the edge of the pool, and ease him in. The magic waters will pierce him. He will leap out and walk away free on his own two legs.

And then it does happen, too late almost to hope for it anymore: someone happens by and has pity on him, on him alone. Only, the one who happens by, the one who has pity, pays no mind to the swampy pool water and its alleged curative powers. He simply issues a brusque command to the man lying on his back: "Get up! Pick up your mat and walk!"

And the man does.

Later that day, the man, now walking, still carrying his mat, gets into trouble with the city's religious gatekeepers. They don't seem to notice the astounding miracle. They do notice, with fierce indignation, that one of their made-up rules has been broken.

They pitch a fit.

That's like having a million dollars flutter through your open window, landing at your feet, and your getting upset because you just swept the floor. It's like having a goose who lays golden eggs waddle into your living room, and your shooing it because it's dropping feathers on the carpet. It's like hearing the town crier yelling at midnight that the invading army has been defeated, and your yelling back to shut up, you're trying to sleep.

But all that man can think about are the words of Jesus: "Get up! Pick up your mat and walk!"

After thirty-eight years. Even if now the man can, in theory, get up, pick up, and walk, he can't do any of it in practice, and won't be able to for a long time. He has no sense of balance. His bones have gone soft. His muscles are spongey. He will need months of physical therapy before he can even totter. If my brother could only barely make it across the room his first time out of bed after his heart transplant, how much more will this man, thirty-eight years on his back, have a long, painstaking rehabilitation?

But no: he gets up, picks up, and walks. Easy as pie.

So the miracle of healing goes all the way down. He is made whole in one swoop: ability and agility all bundled together. All at once, nerves reconnect, muscles turn sinewy, equilibrium is perfectly calibrated, and a hundred other things besides.

The man's healing—the restoration of his *capacity* to walk—and the man's getting up, picking up, and walking—his *actual walking*—are all of a piece. Indeed, Jesus' command is fulfilled in the man's enactment of it. It's not that Jesus first says, "I heal you. Now you can walk. Go ahead, try it. Be careful . . ." He just says, "Walk!" The man's healing is realized by his acting on it. He walks by walking.

Do you see? Jesus commands the man to do the very thing he cannot do, has not been able to do for thirty-eight years, and it is in doing this thing—getting up, picking up, walking—that he steps from no to yes, from the impossible to the possible, from stuckness to freedom.

It is the way Jesus often works: he commands the impossible—be healed, be well, be whole, be loved, be saved—and it is in the moment of our trusting his word that the thing itself becomes possible. Until Jesus said it, commanded it, it wasn't possible. We cannot save ourselves or heal ourselves or make ourselves new or whole or beloved. But then one day Jesus happens by and learns of our condition and has pity on us and asks us if we want to get well, and we whine a little, complain a little, blame a little, and he loses patience with all that and, *bam!* declares us new, well, whole, healed, loved, saved.

We either believe him or we don't. And if we don't, we don't move. We don't act. We live as we've always lived. We lie on our backs and complain that nobody helps us.

But when we do believe him—that we're new and whole and well and healed and loved and saved—and act as though it's true, we find out it *is* true. What he commands he has also made possible.

And so we get up, pick up, and walk.

The healing and the walking are all of a piece.

This is a long way to come to a simple point: there is a hidden miracle in every act of getting up, picking up, and walking. A child the first time she pulls herself up on the edge of a coffee table and lurches toward her mommy; my brother, at the gentle scolding of a nurse, shuffling across the hospital linoleum; a refugee pushing against her hunger and weariness and blistered feet to take one more step, and another: in all these things, we discover over and over the miracle of being pedestrian.

It's as though every day Jesus happens by, learns of our condition, and has pity on us. He listens awhile to our excuses and our accusations, and then grows impatient with all that and turns and says, "Get up, pick up, and walk."

And the healing and the walking are all of a piece.

WALKING TO THE MUDDY RIVER

Second Kings 5 is one of those Bible stories delightful in its oddness. It's about a sort-of pagan from Aram named Naaman. (I say "sort of" because at least one of Naaman's accomplishments is chalked up to divine intervention—2 Kings 5:1.) He's a valiant soldier, we're told, a great man, highly regarded. He has

influence in high places. But all his power and status and great-
ness are being eroded by one thing: he has leprosy. The man is
rotting from the inside. He's falling to pieces.

But then, a rumor of hope. A Hebrew slave girl in Naaman's
household tells him, through his wife, that there is a prophet
in Israel who can do something about his sickness. The prophet's name is Elisha. Naaman uses his influence in high places
and soon enough has secured an audience with Elisha. Sort of.
Elisha doesn't actually come out to meet the great Naaman. He
simply sends a messenger: Walk down to the Jordan River and
wash yourself seven times. That will do the trick.

Naaman is overjoyed.

No. Actually, Naaman is enraged. He pitches a toddler-like
tantrum. He tosses a full-on hissy fit. "But Naaman went away
angry and said, 'I thought that he would surely come out to me
and stand and call on the name of the LORD his God, wave his
hand over the spot and cure me of my leprosy. Are not Abana
and Pharpar, the rivers of Damascus, better than all the waters of
Israel? Couldn't I wash in them and be cleansed?' So he turned
and went off in a rage" (2 Kings 5:11–12).

"I thought that he would surely come out to me and . . . wave
his hand over the spot and cure me of my leprosy."

Translated: I thought he knew how important I am, and also
that this would be quick and easy and dignified.

So Naaman storms off. But his servants—there is a lovely
subplot in this story about the subversive goodness and boldness
of servants, and also about another servant's greed and treachery;
but I digress—Naaman's servants tell him, in effect, *Don't be
an idiot. If the prophet had told you to do something awesome—
rout an army, slay a dragon, swim an ocean—you'd be up and at*

*it. Instead, he tells you to go bathe in a muddy river, and you're
sulking and raging.*

Naaman listens to his servants. He does what he's told: dips
seven times in the muddy river. And it does the trick. He's healed.

The story is about God's restorative power. It's also about
the long, slow, undignified way that even divine healing sometimes takes. Divine intervention is not always quick and easy
and noble. It's also about humility: an important man reduced to
lowly things, to following strange orders from those he otherwise
feels superior to—prophets, servants. *How desperate are you?* the
story seems to ask us. *Do you want to get well?*

And one last thing: the story is about walking.

Naaman travels to Israel in an entourage of horses and
chariots. He waits outside Elisha's door, mounted high in his
chariot, waits for the prophet to come forth and "wave his hand."
Naaman's the CEO who can't be bothered to turn off the jet
engines and descend the stairs to the tarmac. He's too busy, too
self-important. Let the doctor come to me. Let the lackeys attend
to my needs, on my schedule. And if you can't just wave your
hand and make this happen, or give me a pill, at least, at most,
send me to an exotic all-inclusive spa in my own land. How
about the Abana Damascan Club?

But Elisha can't be bothered to even come out his own door
to see the important man. And worse, he sends Naaman to a
muddy river in Israel. To a backwater. To a crick.

Naaman must dismount his horse-drawn chariot and walk
down to that river. He has to stand there, hip-bone deep in the
murky water, and keep plunging himself under, one, two, three,
four, five, six, seven. Only then does he come up clean, his flesh
shiny and taut.

Humility, obedience, submission, trust in the strange ways of God, in the God of strange ways—all this is the stuff of Naaman's healing.

But to get to that place of healing, first Naaman must walk.

I wonder how many times if what stands between me and some healing God wants to do in me—maybe not leprosy but other things that ail me and rot me: anger, sadness, boredom, stiff joints, sore knees, aching back—is simply that I have to step down from my high place and go for a walk.

God Speed

FROM LOST TO FOUND

In her autobiography *Wild: From Lost to Found on the Pacific Crest Trail*, Cheryl Strayed recounts the tale of walking more than a thousand miles, from California to Washington, from desert to mountain, from open land to dense forest, from blazing heat to numbing cold.

From despair to hope.

From, to use her words, lost to found.

She doesn't mean *lost* and *found* in the way Christians use such language. She doesn't mean an "Amazing Grace" kind of lost and found. And yet her story, in a deeply human way, is about grace and redemption and a dead heart coming to life. After Cheryl's mother died, she lost all her bearings. In her grief, she self-destructed. She had multiple affairs and destroyed a good marriage. She pushed her friends away.

She named herself *Strayed*. That seemed the truest thing about her: one who cannot stick to the trail. Who keeps wandering from the chosen path, taking the wrong direction.

And then for no clear reason, and without any experience or training, she decided to walk a thousand miles, mostly through wilderness, and persisted against all odds and sound advice.

It nearly killed her.

It made her alive.

The walking healed something deeply broken in her.

On this walk, probably you don't need to go a thousand miles. But likely there is something broken in you. Maybe it's physical. Maybe it's emotional. Maybe it's a relationship.

Maybe you've strayed.

On this walk, dare to name what it is. And dare to invite God into it, to lead you out of it: from broken to whole, from lost to found, from dead to alive.

Continue, for as many walks as it takes.

CHAPTER 14

Walking as Exorcism

Some while ago, my brother's family and my family, four adults, five children—rented a large beach house for a week on the coast of Oregon. Our stay spanned July Fourth, American Independence Day. I'd never once been in the States during their biggest hoorah, and haven't since. I had no idea what a lollapalooza the whole thing is. Thousands of celebrants, in groups as few as two and as many as a mob, gathered around massive bonfires all up and down the coastline. Many people were well into their cups early in the day. They plunked down lawn chairs and beach chairs, pumped out music from boom boxes, cheered and yelled and sang and danced. As dark descended, the sky was festooned with fireworks. I kept thinking that this would be the perfect time for an alien invasion: no one would see the green men coming. Even their biggest starcraft could move camouflaged amid all the bursting lights; their loudest gun blasts would be drowned out by the concussive bursts of pyrotechnics and the raucous clamor of drunken song. They could rain down wholesale destruction and no one would notice.

My brother and his wife have lived in the US since the midnineties. Both their children were born there. So this was standard issue for them, just another Fourth of July bit of hubbub. But for me and my family, it was pure spectacle. We stood agog.

We stayed up late to watch the whole show and went to bed groggy, slightly rattled, blinking away bright spots in our eyes. We slept until midmorning.

But not my son, Adam. He was thirteen at the time. He awoke early to pull a prank on us. The place we were renting had a garage, which we weren't using. The prank Adam concocted was to steal our van keys, drive our new van into the garage, put the keys back, and then startle us all by running into the house and declaring the car had been stolen. We would all run out, see the van vanished, and then—well, I think the plan was then he would fess up, and we'd all have a good laugh.

This is not how it went. Remember, Adam's thirteen. He doesn't drive. He doesn't know how to drive, though I know for a fact that sometimes an older buddy of his let him get behind the wheel of his junker in empty parking lots.

Adam hangs up three panels of the van on the metal garage door track and gouges the whole thing an inch deep and three feet long. He doesn't then run into the house with any announcement. He makes several vain attempts to remove the damage with a toilet plunger, and then skulks inside and whispers his crime to his mom. His mother then sits me down and breaks the news.

Which I take in with otherworldly serenity.

Well, not quite.

I explode, brighter and louder than one of the Roman candles we'd watched the night before. I am ready to rain down fire. I am about to sell my son into slavery to pay off his debts.

Cheryl tells me I should go for a walk instead.

So I do. I descend grassy silky dunes to the hard-pounded sand along the surf line. I walk south, straight toward a far point, no more than a dark line on the horizon. The beach is strewn with garbage and charred logs from last night's fires. Many of those fires, like me, still smolder hot.

I walk. I walk for miles and miles. The first several are pure rage, broken intermittently with wild anxiety. How am I to pay for this? My insurance will be null and void, because the accident was caused by an unlicensed, uninsured, underage driver. That leaves me to come up with money for what I estimate will be $4,000 in repairs. Or should I lie to the insurance company, say I did it, and live with the guilt of that? Or should I leave the damage unrepaired and bear this ghastly blemish as a mark of my own disgrace?

I start picking up garbage: chip bags, candy wrappers, donut boxes. Not cans and bottles: I figure others will pick those clean later, return them for a deposit. But the other stuff, left on the beach, will sweep out in the next tide and poison and clutter our already poisoned and cluttered oceans.

Stooping, gathering, stuffing smaller things in larger things, heading to one of the garbage bins at the edge of the beach to toss it all in when it becomes too much, then heading back out to collect more. The activity calms me. It is a kind of holy work, collecting and then getting rid of trash.

In my growing calmness, my mind clears—or at least gets clear-ish. My rage ebbs. My anxiety quiets. And God starts to speak to me and show me things. He shows me myself. The picture is not easy to look at: my childish pettiness, not just concerning my son's mistake—that was only a symptom of it—but spreading over and pulsing through almost every area of my life. My lifelong fretting over money. My lifelong struggle with anger. My controlling tendencies. My high expectations of and easy disappointment with others. My ready excuses for myself.

And then it gets worse. I see all the ways this has hurt the people in my life—my wife, my children, my family, my friends, those I work with. It puts them on edge. It erodes their trust.

And then, a memory falls.

I am sixteen, barely. Just two hours before, I have gotten my driver's license, my performance a near-flawless demonstration of my skill behind the wheel. "Congratulations, young man," the adjudicator said as I pulled back into the parking lot at the licensing office. "That was one of the best road tests I've ever witnessed."

Indeed.

I come home elated, flushed, bigger than life. I ask my dad if I can borrow his nearly new company car, a sleek two-toned Plymouth with a V-8 engine (this was the seventies). It is a hot cloudless day in late June. Where can I go? Somewhere I will be seen, admired, applauded.

The mall.

I put on my tightest jeans and T-shirt. I speed along the boulevard. Radio loud. Windows open. Singing. I'm looking around to look at who's looking. One hand on the wheel, light, loose. Barely touching it. My foot bearing down heavy on the gas pedal. The V-8 surging.

These are all things I didn't do in my road test two hours earlier.

I get to the mall, cruise up and down the lines of parked cars looking for a place to park. There's one. One finger in the spokes of the steering wheel, dialing it like an old rotary phone, I spin the car into the spot.

But it doesn't work out that way.

I hang up three panels of the car on the edge of the bumper of the car in the next stall. It gouges a wound an inch deep, three feet long.

I drive home in a trance. I make a vain attempt to repair the damage with a toilet plunger. I whisper my crime to my mother, and then go to my room and crawl into my bed and wait for the fire to fall. My father is often angry in a way that is terrible and terrifying. I want to run away rather than face that. My mother sits my father down and explains what I have done.

And he takes it with otherworldly serenity.

Truly.

He actually laughs about it, and tells me about something similar he did to his father's car as a teenager. "I'm not sure how I'm going to tell the insurance company about this," he says. "But I'll figure it out."[38]

I weep.

And begin to weep now, walking the beach, collecting the trash.

And then a miracle: grace. A cool abundance of grace. It pours out, from God's own hand, it seems. So much grace. So pure. Cascading. No end to it. Grace on grace on grace. Grace from my father. Grace from the Father. Grace drenching down to wash my anger clean. Grace sweeping away my anxiety. Grace buoying me with courage. Grace that is peace like a river.

Hours after setting out, I come back. I find Adam. We stand beside each other, surveying the damage to the van. I tell him about something similar I did to my dad's car when I was a teenager. We laugh. We hug.

"I don't know what I'll tell the insurance company," I say. "But I'll figure something out."[39]

"I love you, Dad," he says.

"I love you too, Son."

It is a kind of holy work, collecting and then getting rid of trash.

CASTING OUT DEMONS

Jesus did quite a few exorcisms—several recorded in the Gospels, many that never made the record, but that are hinted at broadly (for instance, Mark 16:9; Luke 8:2). Casting out demons was central to his mission (for instance, Mark 3:15; Acts 10:38). The stories that got written down are dramatic—demons howling, writhing, knocking about their victims with near lethal violence, begging Jesus not to hurt them. They are a nasty lot, demons. They dig in, with claws and chains. They do their worst. They clear out only under holy assault. None, it turns out, are excited to get to their final abode (for instance, Luke 8:31).

It might help if we paid more attention to these stories. If we took them more seriously. Recently I had a chat with a leading professional theologian who was wondering about how the school where she taught might incorporate a course on "spiritual warfare" while still maintaining academic rigor and theological respectability. "How can we talk about these kinds of things," she asked, "about demons and evil spirits and the devil, and about deliverance and exorcisms and such, and not look wacky and flaky?"

"I understand," I said.

And I do. I have seen damage, some of it minor, some of it deep and wide, done by Christians who lack a sense of proportion in these matters. As C. S. Lewis notes in his book *The Screwtape Letters*, the devil's main strategy is to try to get people to believe in him too much or not at all. Both work equally well for his purposes. The devil can stalk in broad daylight, unopposed, those who refuse to believe in him, who generate "rational" explanations for everything, no matter how twisted or evil, who grasp earthly weapons to fight otherworldly powers. And the devil can tie up in knots those who believe overmuch in him, who ascribe every delay, every disruption, every minor ailment to his personal handiwork, who grasp at supernatural remedies to battle everyday struggles. To explain solely on political, sociological, or psychological grounds an entire nation exploding in genocidal carnage is as foolish and harmful, and flat-out wrong, as chalking up to demonic affliction a two-year-old exploding in a temper tantrum. Both explanations are deficient: the first one gives too little credit to the devil, the second too much.

"Yes, I understand," I said to my professor friend. "But don't you find it surpassing strange that a theological school should have got to the place where it's embarrassed by and lacks theology for understanding large swaths of the New Testament?"

During my years as a pastor, I became a staunch believer in the power of the devil to wreak havoc, and a more staunch believer in the power of God to deal with it. I saw lives ruined, not just by sin but by evil. And I saw lives transformed, not just by God's truth but by his power. So now when I read biblical accounts of demoniacs shouting at, cowering before, pleading with Jesus—and then Jesus tossing them, one and all, down the cellar by the ear—I take them straight up. And when I read biblical accounts of confused or sick or hurting or wayward or hungry people coming, eager or wary, to Jesus, and his meeting them in simple, earthy ways—teaching them, touching them, feeding them, healing them—I take these straight up too.

I don't think Jesus wants to deliver humans from being human. We experience, on more or less a daily basis, anger, sadness, weariness, fear, lust, pettiness, and the like. Or at least I do. These things Jesus tends to do two things with. One, he stands with us in sympathy and solidarity. "I get it," he says. He was, after all, a man of sorrows, familiar with suffering. He was tempted in all ways as we are. He trod the same ground we do, end to end. He knows us, through and through.

He is not ashamed to call us brothers and sisters. He still walks with us in our human weaknesses.

But second, Jesus tells us to go deal with ourselves. He helps, for sure—gives us his grace, his mercy, his example, his Spirit. But he doesn't do for us what we can do for ourselves. *Don't let the sun go down on your anger,* he says (or actually, Paul does). *Be careful how you speak,* he tells us. *Don't look at someone lustfully. Be not afraid.* Clearly, we have some choice in the matter, some influence over how we live and think and feel and act.

What Jesus didn't do was try to cast out anyone's fear or lust or sadness and such. He did not say, "I command the spirit of fear to leave you!" He just said, "Be not afraid." He did not declare, "In my name, I cast out the demon of sadness." He just said, "Do not let your hearts be troubled."

I don't think it's a good idea to attempt what Jesus never tried.

But sometimes Jesus did bring to bear on our humanness not just divine compassion or moral exhortation but divine power.

He brought supernatural remedy to human struggle. Some of the confused, sick, hurting, wayward, hungry people Jesus met needed more than just his sympathy or encouragement.

Some needed deliverance.

Some needed a kind of exorcism.

DIABOLICAL PROPORTIONS

Think of Peter. He declares Jesus is the Christ, the Holy One and Chosen One. Right after this, Jesus—for the first time, as though now he can trust his disciples with grim, weighty matters—speaks to his disciples about the suffering and death that is rushing toward him. Peter will have none of it. He puts on his Big Boss uniform, mounts up his high horse, and in his most stentorian voice starts ordering Jesus around. "Never, Lord!" Peter says, with the force of an imperial decree. "This shall never happen to you!" (Matt. 16:22).

Jesus, just moments before, had lavishly commended, rewarded, and empowered Peter for his heavenly wisdom. "Blessed are you, Simon son of Jonah. . . . You are Peter, and on this rock I will build my church, and the gates of Hades will not overcome it. I will give you the keys of the kingdom of heaven; whatever you bind on earth will be bound in heaven, and whatever you loose on earth will be loosed in heaven" (vv. 17–19).

All this seems, in one wild hot rush, to go straight to Peter's head. He goes from follower to potentate in a heartbeat. He starts exercising his binding and loosing, key-wielding, bedrock powers straightaway.

Jesus' tone with Peter shifts instantly and dramatically: "Get behind me, Satan!" (v. 23).

This is not exactly an exorcism. But it is an acknowledgment that more is going on in and with Peter than a swelled head or a bout of bossiness. It's an acknowledgment that "this kind comes out only" by means other than sympathy and exhortation. It's an acknowledgment that sometimes our human weaknesses swell to diabolical proportions and must be dealt with accordingly.

Or think of the boast Peter makes in response to Jesus' last and most urgent warning about his suffering and death, and his prediction that his own followers will abandon him. This time, Peter is reconciled to the fact of Jesus' imminent suffering and death. But he's certain he won't be counted among the cowards. He'll be the last man standing.

But Jesus tells him, "Simon, Simon, behold, Satan demanded to have you, that he might sift you like wheat, but I have prayed for you that your faith may not fail. And when you have turned again, strengthen your brothers" (Luke 22:31–32 ESV).

Again, this is not exactly an exorcism. It is, though, an acknowledgment that Peter is manifesting not just the usual folly and hubris of the fallen human condition but his readiness to be the devil's dupe and plaything.

Sometimes our human weakness swells to diabolical proportions.

DELIVERANCE

Which brings me back to my long walk on a beach in Oregon and my journey from rage to kindness, from bitterness to gentleness. My rage and bitterness seemed more than a manifestation of my fallen human condition. These things seemed other than mere symptoms of my human weakness. These things seemed . . . well, the most accurate word is diabolical—not mere expressions of my humanness but hideous distortions of it. A power beyond me yet within me took my natural inclinations, amplified them to a decibel just shy of screaming, twisted them into obscene shapes, and paraded them on a pike.

So my walk was more than just a cooling down. It was a coming back. It got me, to use the phrase Mark uses to describe Legion after Jesus deals with him, "dressed and in my right mind" (Mark 5:15). I felt Jesus walking with me, but not just in solidarity. He was not merely asking me to go deal with myself. Rather, he had to tear something out of me, to command something to depart from me, to cleanse something nasty and putrid in me.

He had to deliver me.

I didn't writhe on the ground or froth at the mouth. My eyes didn't roll up into my skull. My head didn't pivot on my neck. I did not spew pea soup. But I came back light, clear, whole. Free.

Dressed and in my right mind.

It's ironic that demoniacs, not disciples, ask Jesus the most poignant discipleship question: "What do you want with me [or us], Jesus, Son of the Most High God?" (See Mark 1:24; 3:11; 5:7.)

Indeed, what does he want with me? With us?

One thing's for sure: to cast out of me these things that would destroy me and those around me. To get me dressed and in my right mind.

I think Jesus did something like this with his first disciples too: cast out of them the things that would destroy them, and those around them. Think of John. His anger seemed something more than human. It seemed beyond him, bigger than him. He needed Jesus, but not only Jesus' sympathy and exhortation: *I get it, John. That must be tough. I'm with you. But you can do it! Just will it away . . .*

John needed something more.

I'm guessing here, of course. But John starts as a "Son of Thunder"—a violent man, an angry man, a loud, petty, selfish, driven man (Mark 3:17; 9:38–41; Luke 9:51–55). By the end, he is the "apostle of love"—a gentle man, a kind man, a wise, quiet, generous, patient man.[40] We have no clear account of how this massive change happened, but my guess is that Jesus helped him by the usual means—kindness, sternness, empathy, an occasional scolding—but also by more direct divine means. John needed, of course, as we all do, the slow patient work of the Spirit, wooing and convicting and reminding and leading him, changing him inch by inch, step by step, by the million infinitesimally small adjustments of the heart that move any of us from one thing to the other. Most of it almost imperceptible except over the long arc of time.

But John also needed some of the Spirit's brusque and abrupt intrusiveness, his invasion into territory claimed by the usurper. John needed the Lord to storm into the corrupt temple of his life, whip in hand, and toss out the moneychangers.

In other words, I'm pretty sure John needed deliverance.

What do you want with us, Jesus, Son of the Most High God?

To get us dressed and in our right minds.

In my case, walking did it.

God Speed

WALKING AWAY FROM OURSELVES

One of my favorite actors is Barry Pepper (a fellow Canadian), and one of his best movies is *The Snow Walker*.[41] Barry plays Charlie Halliday, an arrogant American (just saying) pilot who, in the 1950s, flies his two-seater float plane into remote camps and communities in the Canadian Arctic to deliver supplies. In one camp, an Inuit man pleads with Charlie to take his daughter, Kanaalaq, back to the hospital in Yellowknife. Kanaalaq probably has tuberculosis. Charlie refuses, but the man persuades him by offering him, in exchange, a thick bundle of walrus tusks, rich in ivory. They are worth much money, and Barry's greed is stronger than his apathy. On the flight there, Barry does not acknowledge her except with looks of disgust and annoyance.

They never make it. They crash in the middle of the vast tundra, where stone and lichen and ice and water stretch in endless sameness in all directions. Charlie leaves Kanaalaq—he doesn't even know her name at this point—to fend for herself, and hunkers down with his six-pack of coke and a few cans of Spam and awaits imminent rescue.

Rescue never comes.

And now he is left to fend for himself. But Charlie lacks all notion of survival in the vast, inhospitable land.

Kanaalaq, though, knows how to survive out here. She's done it her entire life. She knows what plants and berries to eat, which ones to avoid. She knows how to skewer fish with a stick and catch birds in a snare and spook reindeer into a trap. She knows how to skin animals and dry their meat. She knows how to tan hides and make them into clothing. She knows how to make shelter out of stone and sod and, later, ice and snow.

She saves Barry's life as her own life fades. They become friends. The final scene—one of the most powerful in the film—is shot at a great distance. Kanaalaq has died and Barry, deeply grieving, buries her beneath a mound of rocks. He continues walking in the direction she was leading him. We see him as a small silhouette, all alone, walking across the snowy plains. Then another silhouette appears: a knot of bodies, maybe thirty people thick, watches him approach. We know they are Kanaalaq's people. He sees them and stops. Last Barry saw them, he could not stand them. Contempt dripped from him. He wanted only to get away from them.

But now he starts walking again, moving toward Kanaalaq's people. All of this we still see from a great distance: a dark speck walking toward a dark circle. He reaches the circle and stops again. And then he walks into the middle of that circle and is folded into it. The two become one.

It's a perfect ending.

The movie portrays not just Kanaalaq's wisdom and grace or Barry's slow humbling and awakening. It portrays not just a tale of courage and resilience and friendship. It shows all that, but also something else: Barry's redemption. Barry's transformation. Barry's being embraced by and embracing those he first rejected.

But maybe, also, it's about Barry's exorcism.

The man needed something torn out of him—his arrogance, his smugness, his bigotry, his greed. His noxious sense of superiority. His selfishness that made him unteachable and incapable of compassion. His independence that rendered him friendless.

Walking did it. Snow walking. Walking with a woman who in every way was his superior but who in no way acted as such.

Barry starts out one kind of man and comes back altogether another. Whole. Light. Free. Cleansed.

Dressed and in his right mind.

A question: How long, how far, might you have to walk to return dressed and in your right mind? What has hold of you that is beyond you and bigger than you, and that all the sympathy and exhortation from others can't seem to make even the smallest dent in?

Or maybe better to ask it this way: What needs to be torn from you? Asked to leave? This is more than just your ordinary human frailty and weakness. It is more than just something that you must bear with, and others as well, until you breathe your last. This is something else. This has roots. This is an occupant. This dwells within you on usurped authority.

Name it and then walk. Walk with Jesus until he says the word. Until it gets behind you. Until the thing departs. Until you are dressed and in your right mind.

CHAPTER 15

Walking as Flight

O urs is a wildly migratory age. So many people unsettled, displaced, on the move. The large-scale pattern of movement is south to north or east to west, but the lines shoot in all directions. Boatloads. Trainloads. Carloads. Caravans. But most of them walking. Weary mothers with children in their stick arms. Bedraggled men with shoes falling off their feet. Gaunt children with dark circles beneath their eyes. Hungry. Scared. Angry. Despairing. Hoping. Seeking an unknown future over a present altogether too familiar.

Why should I care?

Deuteronomy has an answer. In chapter 26 of that book, Moses gives the Hebrew people a reason, both personal and communal, for being generous. Not just freehanded, tipping slightly over the requisite amount, but inside-out generous, overflowing with it. On the surface, the passage is about what I do with my stuff. Underneath, though, it's about remembering who I am. And it's about kindness to strangers.

In the passage, Moses instructs the people to bring God the

first portion, the firstfruits, of their harvests. But he gives a strange reason for doing this. Each Hebrew, tottering beneath the weight of a basketful of their firstfruits, is to enter the dwelling place of God, plunk their offering down, and make a declaration to the priest: "I declare today to the LORD your God that I have come to the land the LORD swore to our ancestors to give us" (v. 3). The next declaration is made directly to God: "My father was a wandering Aramean, and he went down into Egypt with a few people and lived there and became a great nation, powerful and numerous" (v. 5).

God, I'm giving you all this because *my father was a wandering Aramean*. This seems, first glance, rather thin ground for extravagant generosity.

My father was a wandering Aramean. No one knows precisely what this means. Abraham was a wanderer, but not an Aramean. Jacob, too, was a kind of wanderer—at least, he wandered between two homes—and his father-in-law, Laban, was Aramean. But a father-in-law is not a father.

But maybe exact lineage doesn't matter here. *Aramean* seems to be a byword for runaway, fugitive, vagrant, gypsy. The homeless. The vagabond. The man on the run. The guy down on his luck, down to his last crust of bread, shoeless, penniless, reduced to begging or stealing or monkey-grinding. And, besides all that, an outsider. A refugee. Someone with no claim to anything. *My father was a wandering Aramean* means that once I was something very different from what I am now. All this wealth, all this power, all this influence—all this is pure gift. It didn't start this way for me, for mine. It started with my great-great-grandmother carrying her children in her stick arms, the shoes of my great-great-grandfather falling off his feet. So hungry they had almost lost the memory of food.

Never forget this, Moses says. Always remember who and where you've come from (Deut. 26:1–11). All of us, unless you are among the first peoples—Inuit or Blackfoot or Navajo or Quechua and so on—came from somewhere other than here. And few of us were doing well when we arrived. We had, most of us, run out of options. We were starving or under siege or in thrall or being hunted. But we got out (and, alas, tended to displace the people who were already here).

Look at us now: flush, plump, pink, lords of the realm. There we were, a few stragglers, bedraggled, empty-bellied, down to our last filthy ragged shirt, and here we are, a great nation, powerful and numerous.

Always remember, never forget.

I live in Canada, a country many people would love to live in. Safe. Clean. Wealthy. Peaceful. My entire life, I have not once anywhere near my home heard mortar shells exploding or even a gun going off. I once thought I heard a gun, but it was a car backfiring. I once thought I heard an assault weapon, but it was a string of firecrackers. I have never been hungry in a way that I feared for my life, though I have often had a ferocious appetite that drove me to eat until my stomach hurt. I've often complained that I'm starving, but what I meant is that I had gone an hour or two past my regular mealtime. I have fasted long enough to get a blistering headache and feel listless. But I have not once been in danger of collapsing from it.

How did I end up with all this?

I'm not exactly sure. But clearly God has a soft spot for wandering Arameans.

It's odd, then, the resistance I sometimes feel toward other wandering Arameans. Immigrants, we call them now. Yes, it's odd how many Christians are fierce critics and loud opponents—or maybe silent but staunch resisters—of immigration. I'm not talking about whether we need better immigration laws. Most countries do. Every which way we turn, east, west, north, south, the majority world, the affluent West, immigration laws are a mess: tangled in bureaucracy, dizzy with loopholes, chokingly narrow, sloppily loose. Everywhere, reform is needed. Let better minds than mine tackle that.

I'm not talking about that. I'm talking about the spirit in which we think about any desperate person anywhere trying to cross a border. Our border. This mother carrying her child in her stick arms, this father whose shoes are falling off his feet. Their real hunger. The war or tyranny or poverty they are fleeing. The wild hope that draws them.

And God, the God whom maybe they don't know yet, or maybe they do, but who has a soft spot for wandering Arameans. The God who has chosen his church and his people to be his ambassadors. To be his welcoming committee. The God who took a few wandering Arameans and made them a great nation, powerful and numerous, and then said: Always remember, never forget. You too came from somewhere other than here.

ONCE YOU WERE NOT

The New Testament scales this up, wide as earth, high as heaven.

We are those, the apostle Paul says, who "were separate from Christ, excluded from citizenship in Israel and foreigners to the covenants of the promise, without hope and without God in the world" (Eph. 2:12). But now we are, by God's intervention, "alive together with Christ . . . and raised . . . with him and seated . . . with him in the heavenly places" (vv. 5–6 ESV).

We are those, the apostle Peter says, who "once . . . were not a people . . . once . . . had not received mercy." But now we are, by God's invention, "a chosen people, a royal priesthood, a holy nation, God's special possession, that you may declare the praises of him who called you out of darkness into his wonderful light" (1 Peter 2:9–10).[42]

Always remember and never forget where you came from. All of us have humble beginnings, spiritually speaking. We are all wandering Arameans.

The logic is simple: you owned nothing, had claim to nothing, were owed nothing. You were displaced, unwanted, indebted. You had lost everything, yourself mainly. God treated you as an heir anyhow. God lavished upon you one blessing after another. How, then, could you turn around and be stingy toward a God so extravagant? How could you be stingy with anyone? Live your life now with hands held open, arms spread wide.

Remember where you came from. You may have had a great upbringing—love, laughter, abundance. Or maybe not. But the truth is, someone among your forebears was a wandering Aramean. Displaced. On the run. Not wanted. Indebted. Lost everything. There was a time you were without hope and without God in the world. Once, you were not a people. Once, you had not received mercy.

Now, you have it all.

Remember that and never forget it. And then join the welcoming committee.

God Speed

IMAGINARY WALKS

Søren Kierkegaard was odd. The nineteenth-century Danish philosopher's influence is deep and wide, but he himself lived his entire life in Copenhagen, Denmark. His voice is heard around the globe, but his movements rarely took him outside city limits. He never married, though he was engaged to Regine (he called her Regina) Olsen. Though lovestruck, he broke off their engagement within a year of proposing, for reasons unknown, but many of his biographers chalk it up to his tragic view of life, to his melancholia, and perhaps to his general overall oddness.

But the cause of the breakup might have been his father, Michael. Not any demand the father made on his son, but his father's influence on his ways of seeing and thinking. His father carried a crushing sense of guilt from an adolescent impulse where he cursed God. He felt God would make him pay for that. A morbid dread of divine punishment hovered over his entire existence.

It was perhaps the reason Michael never ventured far himself. His wool business was in the Jutland, a good day's travel from Copenhagen, but Michael rarely left the house when he was home. Every day, though, he took his sons Søren and Peter for a walk. Their house was pretty much smack-dab in the middle of the city, and he and his sons sallied forth through its streets, visiting the butcher, the baker, the candlestick maker. Michael would greet them all and urge his sons to do the same. Michael, all down the length of their peregrinations, regaled the boys with stories about the city's inhabitants. It was a delightful daily ritual.

Only, these walks were all imaginary. Michael and Søren and Peter never left the house. They were, every one of them, journeys of pure invention, conjured from thin air.

In one sense, this is marvelous: a father so rich in powers of memory and imagination that he can reconstruct the city and its people whole without stepping into it.

In another sense, it's surpassing strange, maybe pathological: a father living mere steps from reality—real streets, real buildings, real people—who chooses instead shadow, rumor, vapor, and chooses this for his sons as well.

Is a boy like that ever going to marry? Is he ever going to be anything but odd?

Whatever deficiencies Søren's imaginary walks may have bred in him, though, they did nothing to hamper his creativity. Indeed, the walks, I suspect, did much to awaken this. Søren had a prophet's wild brokenheartedness and fierce truth telling. He had a poet's love for wordplay, startling turns of phrase, sideways hints, and an artist's third eye, the capacity to see beauty hidden in the mundane. Søren, like his father, could conjure things unseen.

But maybe the best gift those imaginary walks gave Søren was this: they prepared him for later in life when he walked, daily, physically, in real time, the streets of Copenhagen. Likely the childhood awakening of his imagination trained him to see more vividly what was right before him. "I find," Søren wrote, after the death of his father, Michael, and only a few years before his own death at age forty-two, "a Christian satisfaction in the thought that, if there were no other, there was definitely one man in Copenhagen whom every poor person could freely accost and converse with on the street; that, if there were no other, there was one man who, whatever the society he most commonly frequented, did not shun contact with the poor, but greeted every maidservant he was acquainted with, every manservant, every common laborer."[43]

Søren's imaginary walks prepared him well for the real thing—made him more awake, more attentive, more humble, more curious, more approachable. "The not-quite-real walk," Geoff Nicholson writes, "the walk that doesn't quite take place, that takes place largely or solely in the imagination, that contains an element of fantasy or fraud, is a curious phenomenon and more common than you'd suppose."[44] More common, yes, and perhaps its own kind of awakening, its own preparation for reality.

A way to test this theory, at least in a loose, unscientific way: If first I imaginary walk a path, will I actually walk it, in real time, more awake and attentive? Will imagining it help me see it more clearly, be more present on it?

But why not take this a step—or several steps—farther? This chapter was about remembering that your father was a wandering Aramean, and it was a call to have fresh eyes for this man, this woman, this child displaced by war or hunger or catastrophe, now at your border or now in your town. For this next walk, imagine you are that person—that man, that woman, that child. See your community through their eyes. Feel what they feel. Long for what they long for. Try to step into their uncertainty, their curiosity, their thankfulness.

Walk out your own preparation for reality.

CHAPTER 16

For Those Who Can't Walk

There are several miracle stories in the Gospels where Jesus heals a man—all the stories are about men—who can't walk, and in a couple of cases who can't move at all. There's also a story about a healing like this in Acts, where Peter and John perform the miracle. We'll look at one of these stories in a moment.

Before that, pause with me. Wonder at the wonder of it all. One minute, you can't walk. The next, you can. And not just walk but leap, run, dance. One day, you need to be carried around. The next, you carry things around. One day, the simplest tasks— crossing a room, lifting a cup, scratching an itch—are things you only dream about. The next, you're doing them.

It's the exact opposite of how these things usually go down. What we are familiar with, tragically so, is catastrophic injury that renders a person instantly immobile: one minute they can walk, the next they can't. If there's any coming back from this, it's grueling and painstaking, inch by agonizing inch. There's therapists and therapies and expensive equipment, and months or years of tiptoeing. Jesus' acts of healing, then, are miraculous not only because of the acts themselves but because of their instantaneity, their abracadabra quality.

Shazam! Kaboom! Voila!

None of the gospel writers gives a backstory for those who can't walk. The closest we come is with the man at the pool of Bethesda. John says that he had been in his condition for thirty-eight years and had sought a cure in vain (John 5:5). But that's it. We don't know how any one of them lost use of their legs (and, in those couple of cases, their arms). Falling from a ladder? Thrown from a horse? A childhood disease? A war injury? Any guess is as good as the next.

We do know, from other sources, that it was a terrible hardship for them. It's a terrible hardship now, but the kind of social and medical support that many of us take for granted was not available for working-class people in first-century Palestine. You depended on family, maybe a few loyal friends, the charity of strangers to eke out a bare existence. There were no prosthetics, no physical therapy, no miracle drugs, no medical insurance. On top of that, people often ascribed your condition to your sin. It was your fault. Think of Job's "comforters," or think of the disciples' question to Jesus about a blind man: "Rabbi, who sinned, this man or his parents, that he was born blind?" (John 9:2).

People with physical afflictions were doubly lonely.

So to have Jesus say to you, "Get up!" and then you do—you simply get up, right there, right then—that's good news indeed. Those words, and the power behind them, restored everything: health, work, relationships, reputation.

Where I live, probably where you live, there are systems and programs and trained professionals and insurance to help people with disabilities. And it is rare for anyone to blame the person with a disability for their disability. But I've talked to many people with disabilities, and most are still doubly lonely: not seen, not welcomed, a burden. Few people know how to befriend them. A common story: after the accident or illness that rendered the person disabled, most of their friends vanished. And if no one exactly blames them for their condition, many people make them feel vaguely responsible for it, as though they chose this.

Those who can't walk often have no one to walk with them, no one, other than someone on a payroll, who is simply their friend. No one who meets them for a meal, who takes them to a movie, who visits them just to talk, who travels with them. It's too awkward, too complicated. Even as I write this, I realize that my friendships are based on ready mobility and heightened convenience: meeting in a certain place at a certain time for a certain duration. Being a friend of someone who is disabled complicates all this.

It's slower. Slower even than three miles an hour.

SOME MEN

One story of Jesus' healing a man who can't walk or move has friendship as its subplot. It's the story of a paralyzed man whose friends break a roof apart and lower him down through it. It takes place in Capernaum, Peter's hometown, Jesus' headquarters for his Galilean ministry. It likely was Peter's house, or even Jesus', they were tearing a hole in.

We are not, as I said, told why this man is in this condition. Or how long he's been this way. The story's focus is not really the man at all, or his healing: the man, his healing, simply sets up and gives backdrop to a theological matter, a dispute Jesus has with the scribes about his authority to forgive. But some curious details jump out and some nagging questions pop up.

Like this: who are these friends?

"Some men," Matthew, Mark, and Luke all call them. *Some men*, indeed. There are at least four, we can assume: one on each corner of the gurney. But Mark hints that there are more, that four carry the man, while others run alongside. Matthew says, simply, that they bring the man on the mat to Jesus. But both Mark and Luke note that it isn't that simple, that easy, that straightforward. Jesus is inside a house, preaching, and a huge crowd blocks all entrances. These men, these friends, would be justified in calling it a day. They've tried, they've failed, *c'est la vie*.

But these are *some men*. They are not deterred. The obstacle toughens their resolve. Up they go to the rooftop, perhaps up a staircase but more likely up a ladder, the man on the gurney with them, tottering, teetering, turning at precipitous angles. The men dig through the roof. With bare hands? Clawing through sun-baked waddle and daub? Or maybe they improvise rough tools from sticks and slats and dog bones and bore through? Either way, they vandalize the place. Then, with ropes or some such, they lower the man, gurney and all, though the hole they've made, tottering, teetering, turning at precipitous angles.

It's dramatic, almost comical. There is Jesus, in full cry, expatiating on some grand eternal theme or the next, and suddenly the roof caves in, big chunks of caked mud tumbling down through rafters, dust pluming through the air. Jesus stops. The man, limp on a bed, dangles before him. The men, the friends, peer down through the opening. Maybe they wear worried looks, but I picture them all with rakish grins, like cartoon bank robbers caught in the act. Jesus looks up at them. Maybe he's grinning too.

And then the most astonishing thing happens: "When Jesus saw *their* faith, said to the paralyzed man, 'Son, your sins are forgiven.'" After a brief interruption, Jesus also heals the man: "He said to the man, 'I tell you, get up, take your mat and go home.' He got up, took his mat and walked out in full view of them all" (Mark 2:5, 10–12, emphasis mine).

Their faith. Jesus forgives and heals the man in response to their faith, the faith of some men, the faith of some friends.

This story ends with the paralyzed man walking. Everyone is amazed. Everyone praises God, presumably even the naysayers. Healings like this still happen, and the story inspires us to practice great faith. The deaf sometimes hear, the blind see, the lame walk, the dead are raised.

But in most cases, paralyzed people stay that way.

But this doesn't exhaust what this story calls us to. It also invites us to consider what it means to be the kind of men and women who would do almost anything for a friend with a disability.

Including remaining a friend, even if they never get up and walk.

THE SPEED OF OUR SOULS

A word to those who can't walk. This will be brief and tentative, since I have no idea what that is like. But I risk a word all the same.

Of all the benefits of walking, the greatest one, I think, is slowing down: slowing down to catch up—to get alongside the three-mile-an-hour God, to move at the speed of our souls, to pay attention to the world within and without, to savor moments and presence, to listen well and remember well, to dream afresh.

None of this is the exclusive preserve of those who walk. All these things are available to all, whatever our abilities or disabilities. My impression from my conversations with those who can't walk is that they have learned all this and practice it better than I do. Life has slowed them down. Some of it has passed them by. All have wrestled through a maelstrom of emotion—anger, depression, bitterness, wild hope. All have come to a place of accepting their condition. All have made the best of it.

Their best, it turns out, is good. Very good. In measurable ways, it's better than mine. I use my legs, my arms, and all the apparatuses that arms and legs give me access to and control over—cars, motorcycles, getting quickly on and off buses, trains, planes, boats—to rush. This is my main mode of travel—hurrying. I dash, I bolt, I scurry. My life is a whirlwind.

I have to walk to stop running.

But those who can't walk are already there. They already move at the speed of their souls. God speed.

This may not be much consolation. I'm sure any one of them would trade, in a moment, their life of deeper attention for a medical breakthrough that restored their mobility. I'm sure any one of them would love to hear Jesus say, "Get up!" and then get up.

But most of the gifts of walking are already theirs. And should a miracle occur and they gain back the use of whatever they lost the use of, I think few of them, if any, would ever be in a hurry again.

FULL USE

I think about my friend Norm. He's the man I mentioned at the very start of this book, who broke his neck in a horse-riding accident. He was living a frantically paced life. He managed a department for a large national organization. He traveled widely and regularly. He attended slews of meetings. His life was good but busy—hardly-room-to-breathe busy.

Norm and his wife, Pauline, lived in Southern Alberta, cowboy country. For relaxation, they often spent evenings and weekends riding their horses.

It was a calm warm evening in early June. Norm had a trip overseas coming up and was itching for at least one more ride before he left. After dinner, he and Pauline saddled up. Norm's horse was stoic and squat, the kind you put a rookie on. Slow and low and sturdy. They rode out toward the horizon, savoring the cloudless sky, the wild grasslands, the aspen forests, and, rising behind it all, the snowy soaring peaks of the Rocky Mountains. Coming back, Norm decided to pick up the pace to a slow trot. The field had been freshly tilled. It was perfect for a soft, gentle ride.

Lying out in the field, just ahead, was a flattened cardboard box. Where it came from, who knows. A wind must have blown it there. Norm rode on. But the horse saw that flattened cardboard box, and it spooked. It jumped sideways. Norm, riding easy, tipped over in the saddle, which spooked the horse again. It jumped sideways once more.

Norm fell headfirst. His outstretched arms never broke his fall. He heard a crack. It was his neck.

His whole life changed.

Initially, for the worse. He lost the use of his legs and his hands. Tetraplegia is the technical term. He was paralyzed from midchest down. He had to leave a job he loved and begin a lengthy hospital stay. They had to sell their home, his car, his motorcycle, their horses. They lost some of their friends, the ones who didn't know how to deal with the radical changes in their life. Everything that was once easy, a matter of course, became complicated, a matter of struggle. He did regain his ability to drive, in a van outfitted with a complex and expensive array of hydraulics and levers and such, and with a special chair. But all this put a strain on Norm and Pauline's marriage, which, aside from all their other challenges, they had to work through.

Norm and Pauline eventually moved to the town next to the one I lived in, and they came to the church where I pastored, and that's how I met them.

I have rarely met a man so kind. I'm sure Norm was always kind—I don't think his accident altered the deep structure of his personality. It's just that his kindness now had abundant room and ample time in which to root and flower, to unfold. Nothing about the man was hurried. He spoke with slow and deliberate thoughtfulness. He moved at the speed of his powered wheelchair. He had time, and took it, for people. Many of these were people others avoided. I'm thinking, say, of Gavin. Most people found Gavin manipulative and prone to stretching the truth. Most people gave Gavin short shrift and a wide berth. But Norm, he poured into him. And slowly, because these things always take time, lots and lots of time, Gavin changed. This kind of human alchemy rarely happens if we don't know how to go slow, at God speed.

I know Norm would leap, literally, at the chance to recover the use of his legs and full use of his hands. He would leap to walk again. Through grueling physical therapy and herculean force of will, he has recovered some movement in his legs and can, with much effort and the use of a walker, shuffle short distances. It gives him the feeling of being an *Upright* once more, a term people in wheelchairs use for people who aren't in them.

I have often prayed for the miracle of Norm's complete healing. I have asked Jesus to say to him, "Get up!" and he gets up.

I hope it happens. But if it does, I think Norm will still have time for Gavin.

NO LIMITATIONS, ONLY POSSIBILITIES

One of my favorite movies ever is *Intouchables*, a French film with English subtitles. *Intouchables* (you have to say it with a French accent, flattening and softening all the syllables, so that it sounds like you're pronouncing the make of a fine Burgundy wine) roughly translates as "the untouchables"—those outside the pale, the lowest caste, the riffraff. It also suggests disconnection—lives and worlds that never touch. And it carries a hint of losing one's sense of touch. All these motifs are at play in the movie.[45]

It's about an unlikely friendship. A black felon, Driss, fresh out of prison and with no intention of working, needs signatures from six prospective employers in order to collect welfare. The six signatures prove he's applied for work, he's made an effort. One job he applies for is to be a personal aide and nurse for Philippe, a supremely wealthy man who has become quadriplegic from a paragliding accident. Driss doesn't want the job. He has no qualifications for it. He just wants the signature. He pushes past a long line of qualified applicants to get it.

Philippe takes the forms and tells him to return the next day.

"And you'll sign it?" Driss asks.

"Come back tomorrow."

Driss returns the next day. Philippe hires him. And so begins a remarkable friendship. It changes them both, utterly. Driss is a force of nature. He is unruly in its root sense—unbounded, without rules. Philippe has been coddled and swaddled since his injury and experiences Driss as freedom. One of the first things Driss does is take Philippe for a joy ride in the rich man's Maserati. The car's been sitting idle since his injury, and he's forced to travel strapped down, wheelchair and all, in the back of a sturdy, boxy oversized van fitted with hydraulic lifts and doors big as portals. Driss wants none of that. He plunks Philippe down in the passenger seat of his Maserati, and they go for a burn. It's what Philippe loves about Driss: he pushes him physically, mentally, emotionally. One of the last scenes is the two of them driving to the Swiss Alps—in the Maserati—and paragliding together. Philippe is in his glory.

What instinct made Philippe hire an untrained ex-felon, days out of prison, with no work experience outside of criminal stuff? The answer emerges over the course of the film: Driss doesn't see Philippe's limitations. He sees only his possibilities.

I had an epiphany watching it. Don't burn me at the stake, but Driss is like the Holy Spirit. He blows into our lives as an elemental force—wind, fire, water—and rearranges everything. He becomes our closest companion. And he does in and through us exceedingly abundantly more than what we could ask or imagine. He does this because he has divine power. But just as much, he does this because he has divine eyes: he doesn't see our limitations, he sees only our possibilities.

Philippe would never have met Driss, never been transformed by him, if he wasn't injured. He would have kept living his life of affluence and ease and never thought at all about the limitations of *that* life, the way it separated him farther and farther from himself. His injury, no question, was a tragedy. He lost mobility. He lost (except in his face, especially his ears) all sense of touch. But through his injury, because of it, he ended up in touch with something otherwise out of reach: a friendship outside all the circles he'd ever moved in. If Driss is like the Holy Spirit, it took Philippe's injury to let him in, to turn him loose.

Which makes me wonder: What parts of my *able* self am I not letting the Spirit mess with and call me beyond? Not letting the Spirit in and turning him loose?

Those who can't walk may have the most to teach about how to walk. Only we'll have to slow down to catch up.

God Speed

STILL ME

Christopher Reeve was Superman. And then he was quadriplegic.

In 1977, Reeve landed the role that made him famous—the nerdy rumpled reporter Clark Kent, who becomes, in a whirlwind confined to a phone booth, the dashingly handsome muscle-rippling Superman. Though Superman, unlike Batman or Spider-Man, wears no mask—the only real difference in facial appearance between him and his alter ego, Clark Kent, is that Kent wears thick-rimmed glasses—nobody ever makes the connection, except Lois Lane, and it takes her some time. It's not that Kent and Superman don't bear an uncanny physical resemblance to one another. It's just that they bear no character similarities: Superman is poised, confident, masterful; Kent is jittery, diffident, bumbling.

Reeve went on to make three *Superman* sequels—four movies altogether about the caped crusader. I saw and enjoyed them all.

But in May 1995, Reeve, like my friend Norm, was tossed off a horse. Reeve's accident happened during a steeplechase event in Virginia—he was an accomplished horseman, despite starting late in life. He had just started his course and was thinking ahead to a couple of difficult jumps later in the run. He was not thinking at all, really, about the third jump, an easy, standard three-foot gate. A trained horse and rider could make a jump like that blindfolded. But Reeve's horse made, in the language of dressage, a refusal. The horse stopped dead just before the gate. Reeves catapulted forward, carrying in his hands reins, bit, bridle. He hit the ground headlong. The impact paralyzed him from the neck down. Later, after tricky surgery reconnecting his head to his spine, he regained some movement in his hands and legs, mostly just his index finger on his left hand. He never gave up pursuing fuller rehabilitation.

Reeve went through profound depression. While still in the hospital from the accident, he contemplated suicide. He suggested this to his wife, Dana. "Maybe," he mouthed to her from his hospital bed, "we should let me go." Her answer changed everything for him. "I am," she said, "only going to say this once: I will support whatever you want to do because this is your life and your decision. But I want you to know that I'll be with you for the long haul, no matter what. You're still you. And I love you."

Still you.

Still Me became the title of Reeve's 1998 biography. The title is a poignant play on words. He is still himself. He's still the man, the husband, the father, the actor he always was. But now he is a still version of himself. He is still a man but cannot move. He is still a husband but cannot embrace his wife or feel the sensation of her touch on his body. He is still a father but cannot swim or run or throw ball with his children. He is still an actor. Just not Superman. Not even Clark Kent.

Reeve died at the age of fifty-two, on October 10, 2004. The immediate cause was a heart attack, but the underlying cause was an infection stemming from health issues related to his paralysis and perhaps from his early childhood.

He spent the years between his injury and his death, nearly a decade, as an activist for spinal cord research and an advocate for those with spinal cord injuries. And he went on to direct several award-wining movies and television shows, as well as resuming his acting career. He even appeared in a couple of episodes of *Smallville*, the television show depicting the backstory of Superman.

Reeve's life after his injury inspired many, and not just those with similar injuries. He showed that you could live a full life without full movement, with hardly any movement at all. He showed that you can travel far even if you can't walk there.

Again, I am not the one to give any advice here. I can only guess what it is like to lose the use of my arms and legs. I hope, should I ever suffer such an injury, that I would have the courage and grace to be still me.

And I wonder if that's the heart of it. For those who can't walk, maybe the greatest test is just that: to be you, still you. Or maybe it's a little more. Maybe the gift is to be *distilled* you—a concentrated you, a more focused you, a more intentional you. A you that, though diminished physically, is enlarged spiritually.

I read once an interview with Joni Eareckson Tada, the author, speaker, artist who, at age seventeen, became quadriplegic through a diving accident. She said that she credited her injury with helping her find her true life's calling. Her injury took her to places and led her to work she would never have found otherwise. Injured, she did not remain herself. She lost much, yes. But she also gained much. In significant ways she became more than herself.

Maybe she became her distilled self. I think of Joni's impact in the lives of thousands, hundreds of thousands, maybe millions over the years, and I wonder what might have been lost if she had led a normal life. She became, after her injury, Superwoman.

I'll say it again: I hope I never lose my ability to walk. But should I ever, I hope I am still me. Or even a little more.

But why not aim for that anyway?

On this walk, ask the Lord to show you what a distilled version of yourself would be. And then aim for it.

CHAPTER 17

The Pilgrim's Progress

The greatest allegory in English literature is a toss-up between Edmund Spenser's epic poem *The Faerie Queene* and John Bunyan's Puritan folktale *The Pilgrim's Progress*. I don't know enough to adjudicate between the two, but if I had to pick, it would be Bunyan's work.

Certainly, the story of Christian, an Everyman figure, undertaking a long and treacherous journey from the City of Destruction to the Celestial City has worked its way deep into our collective imagination. Christian faces many perils and distractions along the way. He experiences several small graces and a few miracles. He meets up with various companions, good and bad, some who help him, some who hinder him, some who need his help. The whole thing plays as a dreamscape. In places it is rollickingly funny, in others grimly serious. And though explicitly evangelical in its sentiments and aims, it also speaks to the human condition. Most people, even those with no particular religious convictions, know the book's title and often its author, and many know its storyline. You don't need to share the author's piety to relate to the story's broad themes: life is a journey, often hard and lonely, attended by a motley crew, riddled with distractions, and yet graced by moments of sheer beauty and goodness. It takes courage, wisdom, friends, and much resolve to stay the course. It's easy to lose your way, but you can always find it again.

And this: the journey works best if you have a destination in mind, though the going is slow.

SLOW GOING

At my age, I should be farther along than I am. I shouldn't be so impatient, so quick to judge, so ready to blurt my opinion, so easily rattled. I shouldn't resent delays or savor gossip. I should be kinder and quieter.

But the going is slow.

Most people I meet wish they were farther along than they are. Most wonder why it takes such a long time to learn wisdom and walk in grace and overcome fears and not bear grudges and stop telling fibs and saying cuss words.

There's Cindy, who came to faith at a church camp when she was twelve. She grew up in an abusive home, and the message of God's love caught her up like the tornado that plucks Dorothy's house clean from its moorings and plunks it down in a new world. By week's end, she'd thrown herself in headlong and never looked back. The changes in her were instant and dramatic. She shared her faith with her family, all of whom came to believe, though her mother took years. Cindy became a leader in her church. She went on several short-term mission trips. She married a good and gentle man of faith, and together they've raised four kind and thoughtful children.

Cindy is now in her early fifties and doing well. But a part of her is still angry and controlling, still living out of a wound. She bristles and snaps at any word or tone that remotely sounds like criticism. She gets irritated when her husband or grown children don't do as she says. She long ago forgave her mother, but she still stiffens up around her, becomes nervous, defensive, evasive.

And the going is slow.

There's Tony, whose parents, he says, were "loving and kind." His earliest memory is of the church nursery. It's a good memory. But when he was ten, the neighbor kid showed him a magazine that he'd found in his dad's workshop with pictures of naked women in it. The nakedness isn't what captured Tony, though; the way those women looked at him did. There was a mix of brazenness and shyness, like they wanted his attention but didn't want to scare him off. It made him feel desirable and desired. It awakened in him desire. He couldn't stop looking into these women's eyes. He couldn't get over that feeling.

That led to more and the more led to worse, and over nearly three decades Tony lost the ability to relate to a real woman. He's a good-looking man, and smart and funny and kind, and many women have taken an interest in him. But he falls to pieces trying to talk with any of them. He ends up saying something foolish and awkward, and it sends up warning signals. And soon he's all alone again.

Five years ago, Tony went away for six months to get help. It did help. He came out cleaned up. He doesn't look at those kinds of pictures anymore. He's gained confidence in talking with real women. For the past several months, he's been dating a lovely lady who has her own interesting story. They've started to talk about marriage.

But some nights, he sits and shakes with longing for one last glimpse of the world he's left behind. He knows it won't satisfy him. He knows he'll feel terrible afterward. He knows if he does it, he'll be profoundly disappointed with himself. Still, he shakes with wanting it.

And the going is slow.

Walking is the best language for this. Other things in life can and do happen quickly. You can take a course or even just a workshop and learn a great deal in a short time. You can watch a YouTube video or two in a single sitting and know how to fix the thump in your washing machine or replace a stem valve on a dripping faucet. You can spend an evening browsing Wikipedia and become an expert of sorts on rococo art or the mating rituals of Indonesian birds of paradise or the writing disciplines of Samuel Beckett.

But to trust God fully and love people or to forgive a cruel father or to overcome your fear of failing or your shame at losing— such things may happen quickly, but usually not. Usually these things take a lot of walking.

And the going is slow.

There is hardly a slower method to get somewhere than walking.

I live just a little more than a mile to the center of town, which nestles in a pretty river valley. In the six years I've been here, I've walked to or from the town precisely three times. Only once did I do it for sheer happiness. I was preaching an Advent sermon at a church on the far side of town and thought it would inspire me, plus help me work the sermon into my belly, if I walked the two miles. It took me through a snowy predawn winterscape that was stunningly picturesque—fresh snow on the trees and the ground, bright stars arching above, the blue-green edges of the Bow River starting to feather with ice, my breath pluming white on the air. I thoroughly enjoyed the first twenty minutes. I just had not fully reckoned on the coldness and on how much even a few inches of snow on the ground impedes footfall. I arrived at my destination numb and weary. I think it showed up in my preaching.

The other two times I walked were from sheer necessity. I had to drop off a car for repairs and didn't have a lift home and am altogether too cheap to hail a taxi and our small town is too small for buses. So I walked. I picked up groceries as well and hauled those back with me. As I said, my town is in a river valley, which means my house is up the hill.

It's a steep hill. Its steepness I had barely paid attention to the many times I drove it. I had noticed its steepness that cold winter morning on my way to herald good news, but I was descending the hill that time, grateful for rather than resentful of the pull of gravity. But climbing it now, in sweltering heat this time, laden with two bags of weighty foodstuff—well, that walk, maybe all of a mile and a half, went on and on and on. I arrived footsore, sweat-soaked, bedraggled.

And the going was slow.

THE LONG WAY HOME

Which brings me back to *The Pilgrim's Progress*. Christian walks the whole way, one city to the other. Uphill, a lot. Most shortcuts turn out to be false starts or dead ends or, worse, snares. There is no way forward but the long way. It's one sore foot in front of the other. It's beating sun and pounding rain and howling wind.

And the going is slow.

Bunyan published his book in 1678. Most people, of course, got about then by walking. People of means rode horses, and people of lavish means rode in carriages. But most people were neither and had only their legs and, if they were lucky, shoes. They carried themselves.

Christian walks the whole way. It's a perfect metaphor for faith.

If Bunyan wrote his allegory today, would he still have Christian walk? I like to think so. It makes sense. Walking is a picture of working out our salvation. It's a picture of working faith into the grain of our days, the sinews of our muscles, the marrow of our bones, the rhythm of our breathing. Walking depicts how we get hope deep in our bellies. And submit to the fierce demands of love. And figure out what matters most.

It all comes by walking.

And none of these things—our salvation, hope, faith, love, getting it deep in our bellies, and much else—none of these things is made in a rush. All these come slowly. At about three miles an hour. God speed.

And then one day, you realize you're close to home. You smell it at first, the meat roasting, the bread baking, the hypnotic aroma of pies in the oven. Then you hear it, the music, the laughter.

And then you see it. The road bends down toward the house. The big tree, bigger than you remember, in the front yard is in full leaf and heavy with fruit.

And then you see him. Your father. He's puttering in the garden, planting something. He turns. He shades his eyes against the wide light. He yells and starts running. His arms stretch wide. You had no idea he could run that fast. You had no idea his arms opened that wide. Your mother hears, comes out the door, and starts running too. And your sisters. And your brothers, even the older one. All running.

Now you too are light on your feet. Running now. Running home.

But the going was slow, and it came by walking.

God Speed

SLOW GOD

God is slow.

This is perhaps the most obvious thing about God, though rarely noticed. Of all the divine attributes that we laud or debate, ponder or puzzle over, it's seldom or never we mention God's slowness. Yet nothing about God is more empirically verifiable: he just seems in no particular hurry at all.

It's why, incidentally, I don't have any philosophical objections to the notion of an old earth: why would God be in a fired-up rush to create, say, all the forests of the world—the arboreal, the coastal, the tropical, the Amazonian, the aspen woods, and so on—in a single go when he never seems in any rush afterward, not with any tree or anything else besides?

No, God appears perfectly happy to let things unfold in a painstaking way. He meanders. He plods. He's like the Ents in Tolkien's Middle Earth, never hasty. He's like Roger Moore's James Bond, saving the world from catastrophe but taking his sweet time doing it, cracking one-liners as he goes, waiting until the last possible moment to cut the wire that defuses the bomb, as though waiting until the last possible moment is the whole point of the exercise.

Take, for instance, the exodus. It is the central event in Israel's history and the model for Jesus' redemption of humanity. It demonstrates the mighty power of God to save, no matter how hopeless our situation, how total and brutal the trouble we're in. It displays God's heart for the oppressed. It shows his rule over history. It shows that there is no human system that God cannot dismantle for the sake of the least of these. It's good news for the woebegone and woe-begotten, bad news for all who have a hand in that.

But it takes so long. Using Scripture and genealogies, rabbis have debated how long the Israelites were in Egypt, but it was anywhere from two hundred to more than four hundred years before God raised up Moses to deliver his people from slavery.[46] If God can wield powers like this—frogs falling from clouds, locusts devouring crops, darkness engulfing daylight, but just here, while sunlight dances over there—couldn't he have hurried things up a bit in his rescue of his chosen ones? Why the many years of no show of power at all? And then, why the drama? Why the edge-of-our-seats, nailbiting suspense? Why ten plagues and not, say, three, just to make the point and move on? Why does every event unfold with exquisitely agonizing slowness and only heighten the danger rather than resolve the problem?

Later, God uses a metaphor to capture the whole rescue

operation: "You yourselves have seen what I did to Egypt, and how I carried you on eagles' wings and brought you to myself" (Ex. 19:4).

Eagles' wings? Really? Sure, an eagle is no swallow, swift and darting. An eagle doesn't flit about with blurring quickness. But it's no ostrich, either: galloping, wings askew, trying vainly to get airborne. I live in a part of the world where I see eagles, mostly bald eagles, on a daily basis. Their flight is pure poetry. It is high art. An eagle takes to the air with martial command and rides the winds like Zeus. It rarely seems in a hurry, that's true—up there in its lofty heights turning wide circles—but it never seems slow, either.

Maybe after Israel busted out of Egypt, the events all compressed in their memory and it did, indeed, feel like one elegant, breathless ride, a smooth arc from suffering to freedom. But in the moment, on the ground, with frogs raining down around them and still no movement up at the king's house, I think everyone's inner dialogue must have been a single refrain: *How long, O Lord?*

I could sketch out many other biblical stories similarly— desert wanderings, settling the land, exile and return, waiting for the Messiah.

Nothing here happens fast.

Especially, think about making a disciple, just one disciple. Think about it personally. Think about you. Think about the slowness, the laboring, groaning, back-and-forth slowness of it, the many plodding years, the many lapses and mishaps and detours. It's taken all this time for you to become even halfway kind or generous or truthful or loving or just. And how many times have you gotten stuck—in resentment, in fear, in scarcity thinking, in apathy?

Or am I just talking to myself about myself? This sometimes happens.

If not, if some of what I describe also describes you, then the question is, How so? Why so? An easy, and mostly correct, answer is we ourselves are the problem. We sabotage our own flourishing. I've done this often enough not to argue otherwise. But I also think that the slowness of personal formation appears to be universal, something that recovering meth addicts and reformed porn stars struggle with, but so does everyone. Mother Teresa and Billy Graham and the apostle Paul all took a while to become themselves. I think the slowness is built in. It's a *designed* flaw, something God mixed in to the human condition on purpose. He seems to have rigged it. Becoming like Jesus doesn't happen quickly for anyone.

The way we usually account for our slowness to become like Jesus, as I mentioned, is by simply laying all the fault at our own feet. It's our sin, our waywardness, our stubbornness that keep us from getting to saintliness sooner. Again, no argument from me.

But is that the whole story?

Doesn't the sheer universality of our slowness suggest that something else is also at play? I have a guess what that might be: God made people to grow slowly. With most animals, God designed them to go from babyhood to adulthood in a year or so. A chick that comes twitching and gaping out of its shell one week is flitting and swooping on air the next. A puppy that's womb-smeared and blind on Monday, flopping about trying to find its mother's teat, is bounding after a cat a couple of weeks later, and soon after that eating everything it can scrounge. But a human child? Even seventeen or eighteen years on, she's still growing into her limbs, settling into her brain, navigating her emotions, learning to soft-boil an egg.

As in the physical, the emotional, the intellectual, so in the spiritual. We are made to mature at a snail's pace. Though snails, of course, mature much faster.

Maybe I'm making excuses for myself. But maybe not. I think God designed human maturation to be a long arc. But why? Why don't we grow up all in a hurry, like cats?

I am not entirely sure. I just know my own growing happens at about three miles an hour, at God speed, and more and more I need slow down so that I can catch up.

On this last walk from this book, take a familiar route, but go slow. Reflect on the journey your life is. What's come quickly? What's taking a long, long time? What part of that long, long time—that slowness—is self-sabotage? And what part is simply God's way of growing you?

In everything, God speed.

Conclusion

Keep Walking

We've come to the end of the book. But we've not come to the end of the road.

A good book, like a good story or a good sermon, is not done when it's over. After the last page, the book—if it has any merit at all—still lingers, troubles, tickles, woos. It keeps bringing things to us and demanding things of us. That's how Jesus' parables work: not one is done when it's over. The parable of the prodigal son, say, leaves me standing in a field at nightfall, smelling prime rib, hearing clapping and singing inside the house, deciding whether to go in and join or stay outside, wrapped tight in my impressive uprightness, and sulk. The parable of the seeds and soils leaves me pondering the same word it begins with: *listen!* I am left hanging, choosing to listen or not, to till deep my own soil or not. Even a small parable, with no real storyline, needs us to finish it. Think of that batch of odds and sods in Matthew 13, the kingdom-of-God-is-like parables. The kingdom is like plants that grow among weeds. It's like a net that drags in a weird assortment of things. It's like a merchant hunting down a rare pearl. It's like a treasure buried in a field that someone stumbles on.

Seed and weeds. Net and hodgepodge. Merchant and pearl.

Buried treasure and lucky finder. But what's it all mean? These little fragments don't really explain themselves.

It's because not one is done when it's over. Each one needs picking up, turning over, mulling over, wondering at. Each implies, however vaguely, a choice. The choice isn't how to save myself. But it might be how do I become softer soil, with ears to hear? How do I thrive among noxious weeds? How do I search for treasure or make it my own if I stumble on it? Or am I the treasure? Am I the pearl the merchant spends his lifetime looking for and his fortune acquiring? Am I buried riches that someone stumbles upon and then spends his whole life-savings just to make his own?

All's to say, every parable you hear needs you to finish it.

So it is with this book. I wrote it. You've read it, to the end, I'm assuming. Thank you. I am grateful and humbled. Finishing a book is the first test of a book's worth. But the second test is that you finish it in this other way I'm describing: take what is here and complete it. Make it your own.

What I'm saying is, keep walking.

God speed.

Acknowledgments

I found two ironies, both awkward as sticks in my pocket, writing a book on walking.

The first: writing about walking made all my walking self-conscious. Over the course of crafting this book, I became a bit like the man who can't sleep because all he thinks about is sleeping. Almost every step I took, even up and down the stairs or out to the garage, I analyzed, and sometimes the analysis robbed the walking of its naturalness. Can one derive the many benefits of walking—physical, emotional, relational, soulish—if one is thinking overmuch about the walking itself, if one is not, in effect, a thoughtless, careless walker?

The other irony: the days I wrote I barely walked. I sat. I ruminated but didn't peregrinate, and ended up writing stuff like *ruminate* and *peregrinate* where simpler words would have done the trick. I tried to wax poetic and philosophic on the act and meaning and benefits of walking, but I did so motionlessly. In my idleness, I commended action; in my sedentariness, vigor. I was the unmoved mover, but a runtish version of that. Well, I don't know how else I might have done it. I suppose I could have walked and made recordings on my phone, but I did that once and when I played it back, I sounded garbled and winded, like I was escaping zombies.

But aside from these deficiencies, I have thoroughly enjoyed myself these past many months. I wrote this in the midst of life and life to the full—by which I mean, I was mostly busy. I traveled. I spoke in various places. I taught classes. I made some furniture. I ate some good food and some so-so food, but not once got sick from it. I drove, a lot. I rode my motorcycle, not enough. Once, I went down wild rapids in a Zodiac and got so cold I thought I had hypothermia. Another time, I descended a thousand feet of mountain through a set of increasingly harum-scarum ziplines and rappels. Both times, I lived to tell the tale.

But among all this, I wrote. It is a relentlessly tedious and solitary act, writing. It's a bit like being under house arrest, not that I know anything about that. Honest. But there I am in my man cave, pounding the keyboard in my cavemanish way (I never learned to type properly, so my hunt-and-peck method resembles whack-a-mole more than piano flourishes), sometimes staring blankly at the blank wall, hoping it cracks open and words spill out. Above all, I am all alone. Occasionally, Cheryl slips catlike down the stairs to fetch something from the storage room. But she never speaks.

And yet for all my relentless solitariness, I did not write alone. A small village stands behind the completion of what you now hold.

First, thank you to my colleagues at Ambrose University who recommended me for a teaching award, and for the anonymous donor who provided that award, and for Dr. Pam Nordstrom, VP of Academics, who allowed me to use that award not in the way I was supposed to but instead to go to the mountains to write for a week. I wrote almost half the book that week, plus I was as happy as a mountain goat on a wild crag. Very kind of all of you.

Thanks to my friend and former pastoral colleague Rob Filgate for coining the phrase "God Walk" (he spells it GodWalk). We used it for several years as a title for our church's discipleship ministry. Thanks, Rob, for kindly letting me use it for this book.

And there are all the book-making people. Ann Spangler has been my friend and agent now for twenty years. I remember well the day she first called me, in the winter of 2000. Cheryl said a lady from Michigan was on the phone asking for me. I didn't get many calls from exotic places like Michigan back then—or now, for that matter—so I was curious. The lady was Ann, a big-time literary agent who handled big-time authors, and she wanted to know if I wanted her help to get published. This was as astonishing as an angel showing up in my living room. Ann and I struck up a partnership and friendship that day that has carried on now through this, my ninth published book. Ann, you have been a good walking companion. Thank you.

There are the folks at HarperCollins/Zondervan, my publisher now for many years. They're a great team—skillful, professional, dedicated, personable. Thank you. Thanks especially to my editor, Carolyn McCready. She's big time, too, and brilliant at what she does, if at times a tad heartless: so many of my beautiful words, pages and pages of them, she took out to the woods and summarily executed and left them there for the wild animals. But I'm not bitter. I never liked those pages anyhow, or any of the words they contained, and my life is freer and happier without them. So I'm grateful. Truly, Carolyn, you have been a good walking companion, and this book is leaner, lighter on its feet, and more apt to go the distance for your keen eye and sharp knife.

Thanks as well to Brian Phipps, who expertly copyedited these pages. It's the second time he's rendered me such service. Frequently he made me wince with shame—how often, for instance, he hunted down and banished trite and needless phrases ("in other words"—I vow never to use it again). I applaud your ruthlessness, Brian. I only hope there is a room in heaven where deleted commas dwell: thanks to you, I now have many, plucked loose from sentences they once lovingly embroidered, curled up like frightened children, awaiting our reunion.

Three people read early drafts of this book. My colleague Sandy Ayer read the manuscript end to end in a few days and provided many insightful remarks and judicious edits. My "I drive everywhere" friend, Lee Eclov, who said nice things about it but also said it failed to convert him. And my wife, Cheryl, also read the whole thing in almost one swoop. She said it was good—a completely unbiased evaluation—but also handed me three pages of corrections. Others listened to portions of the book as I read them aloud and made cheering and approving noises, or at least polite ones, which I took to mean I was roughly heading in the right direction. To all, thank you.

Several friends have walked beside me these past few years and encouraged me in a thousand ways. In no particular order, thank you, Rob McKinley, Kevin Green, Craig Traynor, Norm DeWitt, Lee Eclov, Doug Ward, Tim Pippus, Ian Byrd, the Inklings (aka the walking gang), Ken Shigematsu, Graham and Anneke Bruce, Ken and Jo-Ann Badley, Gordon and Joella Smith. A shout-out to Jennifer Singh, our "sister and priest," even though she can never remember the title of this book and routinely calls it "your walking thing."

Also, special thanks to Norm Dueck and Graham Bruce for each letting me tell part of your story.

Then there are my three children, Adam, Sarah, and Nicola, who have always made me inordinately happy. They are all now adults and have become good friends. I like nothing so much as walking with them, all at once or one at a time. Even though none of them spoke a word of advice to me about writing this book, their inspiration is all over it. They were on my mind during every walk I document here, and all the ones I don't (Sarah, thanks for the great walks recently in Kaohsiung, Taiwan, especially up Monkey Mountain. Never thought we'd reach the top). When Cheryl and I walk together, a portion of it is always talking about and praying for them. My joy in them soaks every word here. Adam, Sarah, Nicola, you are the reason I walk. I love you. Thank you.

And there is, there has always been, my BMW (Beautiful Marvelous Wife), Cheryl. When I published my first book twenty years ago, we were, it seems, still newlyweds. It's not the case now. But I love you more than ever and find you more beautiful and marvelous than ever. I am dazzled by what God has done and is doing in and through you. You are and will forever be my favorite walking companion. We have covered a lot of miles together. I'm praying we're just getting started. I thank you and love you with all my heart.

Notes

1. Quoted in Geoff Nicholson, *The Lost Art of Walking: The History, Science, and Literature of Pedestrianism* (New York: Penguin, 2008), 1.
2. Rebecca Solnit, *Wanderlust: A History of Walking* (New York: Penguin, 2000), 10.
3. From Brian McLaren, *Finding Our Way Again: The Return of the Ancient Practices* (Nashville: Thomas Nelson), 1–3.
4. See www.humanorigins.si.edu. In 2017, some fifty bipedal footprints were found in Trachilos, Crete, that date back nearly six million years, but their species origin is hotly debated. The oldest set of bipedal footprints in the UK, the Happisburgh footprints, were discovered in 2013 on a shoreline in Norfolk, England, and date to about 800,000 years ago. The oldest ones discovered in North America, on Calvert Island in British Columbia, Canada, date to around 13,000 years old.
5. "[S]pending your whole life on two legs [is] a downright odd thing to do. Plenty of mammals stand on two legs once in a while, but humans are the only ones ridiculous enough to do it all the time. The body just wasn't designed for it. All those bad backs and knees and feet and hips—we'd have had none of those things if only we had remained on all fours. If a quadruped missed a step with one foot, there were three others right there to make up the difference. What was the big deal about

bipedalism, anyway? . . . By some accounts, walking itself was a series of falls, a precarious balancing act that had the walker standing on one leg for most of the time, constantly pitching himself forward, transferring energy and weight in a reckless and dangerous manner, avoiding disaster only by constantly getting a foot down in the very nick of time" (Nicholson, *Lost Art of Walking*, 7–8).

6. Virtually every religion has a tradition and practice of pilgrimage. For the sake of time, space, and theme, I confine myself here to the Christian tradition and practice.

7. Up until 1170, when Becket was murdered, maybe at the behest of King Henry II, in Canterbury Cathedral, the most popular shrine and pilgrimage site in England was St. Swithun's shrine in Winchester. Becket eclipsed him, but why choose? The Pilgrims Way traverses the 120 miles between the two.

8. Benedict XVI, "Visit to the Cathedral of Santiago de Compostela: Address of the Holy Father Benedict XVI," speech, Santiago de Compostela, Spain, November 6, 2010, https://w2.vatican.va /content/benedict-xvi/en/speeches/2010/november/documents /hf_ben-xvi_spe_20101106_cattedrale-compostela.html.

9. Another compelling source of information about these schools is the novel, and subsequent movie, *Indian Horse* by late Canadian writer Richard Wagamese. When my wife and I saw the movie, in a small theater in Banff, Alberta, with about thirty people in attendance, we were all stunned silent by the end. It is the only movie I have ever been to where the audience, to a person, sat mute until the very last credit rolled, and even then we were hardly capable of speaking or moving.

10. Carleigh Baker, "Review: In Must-Read *The Reason You Walk*, Wab Kinew Chronicles His Father's Life and His Own," *The Globe and Mail*, October 9, 2015, https://www.theglobeandmail .com/arts/books-and-media/book-reviews/review-in-must-read -the-reason-you-walk-wab-kinew-chronicles-his-fathers-life -and-his-own/article26741831/.

11. Wab Kinew, *The Reason You Walk* (New York: Viking, 2015), 262, 268. In case you haven't picked up on my enthusiasm for this book, I commend it to you; a crucial part of Cheryl's and my transformative journey for the past fifteen years has been walking out healing and reconciliation with First Nations people.

12. The bitterly funny movie *Smoke Signals* has a hilarious scene that spoofs non-native fascination with native traditions. Worth a watch.

13. See James Arthur Ray's story in Wikipedia, https://en.wikipedia .org/wiki/James_Arthur_Ray.

14. A few: *The Way* (2010); *Walking the Camino: Six Ways to Santiago* (2013); *Camino de Santiago* (2015); *Strangers on the Earth* (2016); *Looking for Infinity: El Camino* (2017).

15. Solnit, *Wanderlust*, 6.

16. Trevor Herriot, *The Road Is How: A Prairie Pilgrimage through Nature, Desire, and Soul* (New York: Harper Collins Canada, 2014), 16–17.

17. *Every Body Walk!* documentary, Everybodywalk.org, YouTube, posted April 22, 2016, https://youtu.be/6-NpTd3J7tg.

18. Dr. George L. Meylan, a Columbia University physician and president of the American Physical Education Association, quoted in Eva M. Selhub and Alan C. Logan, *Your Brain on Nature: The Science of Nature's Influence on Your Health, Happiness, and Vitality* (Toronto: Harper Collins, 2014), 107.

19. Selhub and Logan, *Your Brain on Nature*, 118–19.

20. A sample of US government research on phytoncides: Q. Li, M. Kobayashi, Y. Wakayama, et al., "Effect of Phytoncide from Trees on Human Natural Killer Cell Function," *International Journal of Immunopathology and Pharmacology* 22, no. 4 (October–December 2009), 951–59, https://www.ncbi.nlm.nih .gov/pubmed/20074458; a popular article on phytoncides plus other benefits of being in nature: Qing Li, "'Forest Bathing' Is Great for Your Health: Here's How to Do It," *Time*, May 1, 2018, http://time.com/5259602/japanese-forest-bathing/.

NOTES

21. A sample: Alexandra Sifferlin, "Why Spring Is the Perfect Time to Take Your Workout Outdoors," *Time*, March 30, 2017, http://time.com/4718318/spring-exercise-workout-outside/.

22. I am well aware of the growing body of scholarship that argues their relationship was sexual. The evidence for this is slight at best.

23. Mark Buchanan, *Spiritual Rhythm: Being with Jesus Every Season of Your Soul* (Grand Rapids, Mich.: Zondervan, 2010), introduction and chapter 1.

24. Job 30:1, where Job refers to "the dogs of my flock"—sheepdogs—might be an exception, but Job uses it in a disdainful way.

25. There are two references in the apocryphal book of Tobit where a friendly happy dog shows up twice. Whole books have been written about that dog.

26. The single biblical reference to David's mother—tradition has her name as Nitzevet—is in 1 Samuel 22:3, where David, maybe in his early twenties and on the run from King Saul, places his mother and father in the care of King Mesha of Moab to get them out of Saul's reach. Much speculation, particularly in rabbinical writings, has been generated about her. One talmudic tradition has David as the illegitimate child between Jesse and a household servant girl. But nothing is known for sure. One possibility is that David's mother slipped into chronic postpartum depression after his birth, or the birth of one of his two (perhaps) younger siblings, and played a marginal role in his upbringing.

27. *Luther's Works*, vol. 54, *Table Talk*, pp. 37–38, May 18, 1532.

28. Mary Oliver, "The Summer Day."

29. Though, alas, my wife went to Paris on a girl trip a few months after I went on my boy trip, and came back with the sad news that the locks are all being shorn and removed. Their weight is putting the bridge railings under too much strain. Ah, the weight of eternal love.

30. I recently walked Manhattan again, up and down, side to side, over four days with my wife—and ditto.
31. Eugene Peterson, Regent College, I believe in summer 1993. I agree Annie Dillard's many books are well worth reading. My favorites: her autobiography *An American Childhood*, her novel *The Living*, and her memoir of sorts *The Writing Life*.
32. Alan Castel, "10,000 Simple Steps to a Better Memory: Take a Walk," PsychologyToday.com (January 9, 2014), https://www.psychologytoday.com/us/blog/metacognition-and-the-mind/201401/10000-simple-steps-better-memory-take-walk.
33. Robyn Davidson, *Tracks: A Woman's Solo Trek Across 1,700 Miles of Australian Outback* (New York: Vintage, 1980), 191–92.
34. Tradition locates the starting point of Jesus' last walk at the Praetorium or the Antonia Fortress, but many archeologists have disputed this. The end of the walk is the Church of the Holy Sepulchre, built on the site traditionally identified as the place of Christ's crucifixion.
35. An average estimate of the weight of the crossbeam.
36. Solnit, *Wanderlust*, 50.
37. Tom Wright, *Mark for Everyone* (London: SPCK, 2001), 16.
38. Three days later, my dad was the victim of a hit-and-run when a dump truck sideswiped him swinging around a corner. He was uninjured. The car? The three panels I damaged were destroyed and the entire car was a write-off under full insurance.

    There is a God.
39. When we got back home, I found a retired body man who had set up shop in his back yard. He repaired the whole thing to a professional standard—for $500.

    There is a God.

    I also made Adam pay me back over the next three years, mostly from money from his paper route. I put the money in a special savings account. Then, when he turned sixteen and could drive legally, I surprised him and gave him the money toward professional driving lessons.

40. This was the traditional designation for John, who is attributed with the authorship of the gospel of John, the epistles of John, and Revelation.
41. *The Snow Walker,* directed by Charles Martin Smith (First Look Media, 2003).
42. With beautiful irony, Peter addresses his letter to "God's elect, exiles scattered throughout the provinces." In Christ, we are both elect (those who are now a people) and exiles (people scattered).
43. Søren Kierkegaard, *The Point of View of My Work as An Author: A Report to History,* written in 1848, published in 1859 by his brother Peter Kierkegaard. Translated with introduction and notes by Walter Lowrie (New York: Harper Torchbooks, 1962), 48–49.
44. Nicholson, *Lost Art of Walking,* 245. Nicholson recounts the strange feat of Albert Speer, the repentant architect in Hitler's inner circle, who, while a prisoner for war crimes in Spandau, walked from "Berlin to Heidelberg" as a sheer act of imagination, though he did the actual walking. He calculated the distance between the two cities and then mapped out a 270-meter circuit in the prison yard and walked it 2,296 times. After he completed that, he carried on to "Munich," and from there to other places, tramping 3,326 kilometers altogether, round and round within the same gray walls, the same dismal surroundings. He was helped in his calculations by his prison mate, the unrepentant Rudolf Hess, Hitler's deputy fuhrer until his capture and arrest in 1941.
45. An English-language version of the movie, called *The Upside,* came out as I wrote this. I have yet to see it, but the reviews I've read claim it holds no candle to the original.
46. David Glatt-Gilad, "How Many Years Were the Israelites in Egypt?" TheTorah.com, accessed March 28, 2019, https://thetorah.com/how-many-years-were-the-israelites-in-egypt/.